# Long Term Care For Retirees

## How to Plan and Pay for the Best Quality Healthcare

By Jeff Weidner
Boom Retirement Solutions

Published by Boom Retirement Solutions
Wake Forest, NC



**Limited Liability and Disclaimer of Warranty:**
Every effort has been made by the author and publisher to ensure the accuracy and completeness of this book. However, the publisher and author make no representations or warranties of any kind, express or implied, about the accuracy or completeness of the contents. They specifically disclaim all implied warranties of merchantability or fitness for a particular purpose.

The strategies and advice in this book may not be suitable for every situation. Neither the author nor the publisher shall be held liable for any loss of profit or other damages, including but not limited to special, incidental, consequential, or other damages arising out of the use or misuse of the information provided. Readers should consult with a qualified professional for personalized guidance.

**Description:**
**First Edition**
Published in Wake Forest, NC by Boom Retirement Solutions, 2025
**Summary:**
This guide reveals the essential strategies for retirees to navigate long-term care planning, protect their assets, reduce tax burdens, and ensure financial security in their later years. Discover how to minimize healthcare costs, plan for future needs, and secure peace of mind for you and your family.
**Author:** Jeff Weidner

**Dedication**

To all those approaching retirement, may you find the confidence and clarity to make the most of your retirement assets, exercise daily, stay healthy, reduce your taxes and create the retirement you deserve.

And to my family, whose support made this book possible.

Download your Free Book

**https://books.jeffweidner.com/free**

SCAN ME

DOWNLOAD FREE BOOK

**Acknowledgments**

Writing a book about long-term care for retirees that is both comprehensive and accessible requires the support and contributions of many individuals. I would like to express my heartfelt gratitude to:

**My clients**, whose questions, concerns, and personal stories provided the foundation for this book. Your trust in me to help you navigate the complexities of long-term care planning has been both a privilege and a source of inspiration.

**The team at Boom Retirement Solutions**, whose unwavering dedication to serving clients with care and professionalism makes our mission impactful. Your commitment to helping retirees plan for long-term care and secure their futures drives everything we do.

**My mentors in the financial services and retirement planning industries**, who have instilled in me the values of integrity, lifelong learning, and putting clients first. Your wisdom has been instrumental in shaping the guidance shared within these pages.

**The editorial team**, whose attention to detail ensured that this critical subject matter is presented with clarity and precision. Your efforts have made this book more accessible and helpful for readers.

**My family**, whose patience, encouragement, and support throughout the writing process were invaluable. You gave me the strength to persevere through the countless hours of research and writing.

And finally, **to you, the reader**, for prioritizing your long-term care planning and taking proactive steps to secure your future. Your commitment to preparing for retirement with confidence and peace of mind is commendable.

Thank you all for your contributions and support, which made this book possible.

**How to Use This Book**

Planning for long-term care can feel overwhelming, but this book is designed to make the process simpler, clearer, and more actionable. Whether you're just starting to think about your long-term care needs or you're ready to finalize your plan, this guide will help you navigate every step. Here's how to make the most of this book:

**1. Start with the Big Picture**

Begin by reading the introductory chapters to understand the fundamentals of long-term care and why it's a critical part of retirement planning. These chapters set the stage by explaining the challenges retirees face and the benefits of preparing early.

**2. Identify Your Needs**

Each retiree's situation is unique. Use the self-assessment tools and case studies provided to pinpoint your personal care preferences, budget considerations, and family dynamics.

**3. Explore Your Options**

Dive into the detailed explanations of long-term care solutions, including insurance policies, hybrid annuities, Medicaid planning, and other strategies. Compare the pros and cons of each option to see what fits your circumstances best.

**4. Take Action**

This book is designed to help you move from planning to implementation. Use the step-by-step guides to start creating your long-term care plan, from calculating potential costs to selecting the right products and services.

**5. Refer Back as Needed**
This book is a resource you can revisit at any stage of your retirement journey. Keep it handy for quick references, such as understanding policy terms, navigating changes in healthcare laws, or exploring new tools and strategies.

**6. Discuss with Family and Advisors**
Planning for long-term care isn't something you need to do alone. Share what you learn with family members or trusted financial advisors to ensure your plan aligns with your goals and their needs.

**7. Use the Checklists and Worksheets**
Practical tools like checklists and worksheets are included to help you stay organized and make informed decisions. These resources will guide you step by step in building and maintaining a comprehensive plan.

**8. Stay Informed**
The world of long-term care is always evolving. While this book covers the most up-to-date information available, stay proactive by consulting professionals and reviewing your plan regularly.

By following these steps, you'll gain clarity, confidence, and control over your long-term care planning. Remember, this book is more than just information—it's a roadmap to ensure your retirement years are secure and your future needs are met.

# Table of Contents

## Introduction

Sarah never expected to become a caregiver at forty-five. Like many Americans, she thought her parents' retirement savings and Medicare would cover any care they might need in their later years. But when her father suffered a severe stroke, followed by her mother's early-onset dementia diagnosis, Sarah faced a stark reality: the system she thought would protect her family had significant gaps, and she wasn't prepared to fill them.

This scenario plays out in countless homes across America every day. According to the U.S. Department of Health and Human Services, nearly 70% of individuals turning 65 will need some form of long-term care during their lifetime, with women needing care for an average of 3.7 years compared to 2.2 years for men. Yet, only about 16% of Americans over 65 have a long-term care insurance policy, leaving the vast majority exposed to significant financial risk.

The truth about long-term care in the United States is both sobering and urgent: our traditional retirement planning methods no longer adequately address the complexities of extended care needs. As medical advances help us live longer, the likelihood of needing some form of long-term care increases dramatically. Yet most Americans remain dangerously unprepared for this financial and emotional challenge.

This book serves as your comprehensive guide to understanding and preparing for long-term care needs. Whether you're in your forties planning ahead, in your sixties considering immediate options, or already navigating the care system for a loved one, you'll find practical, actionable information to help you make informed decisions.

Throughout these pages, we'll explore the rapidly evolving landscape of long-term care, from the disappearing "three-legged stool" of retirement (Social Security, pensions, and personal savings) to the real costs of various care options in 2025. We'll examine why Medicare, contrary to popular belief, covers far less than most people assume, and why family caregiving—though often the default option—may not be sustainable for future generations.

You'll learn about the full spectrum of care options, from home health services to assisted living facilities, and understand the pros and cons of each. We'll delve into various funding strategies, from traditional long-term care insurance to innovative hybrid products, and explore how to protect your assets while ensuring quality care. For those with limited resources, we'll discuss Medicaid planning and other alternatives.

This isn't just another financial planning book. Through real-life case studies like the Johnson family's experience, you'll see how proper planning—or the lack thereof—can impact families both emotionally and financially. You'll learn from others' mistakes and successes, gaining practical insights into what works and what doesn't in various situations.

We'll also tackle the crucial but often overlooked aspects of long-term care planning: how to start difficult family conversations, how to evaluate care facilities, and how to coordinate care among family members. You'll find specific guidance on home modifications, caregiver support, and navigating the complex healthcare system.

Perhaps most importantly, this book will help you understand your personal risk factors for needing long-term care and guide you in creating a customized plan that fits your circumstances. Whether you're concerned about your own future needs or those of your aging parents, you'll find tools and strategies to help you prepare effectively.

The landscape of long-term care is changing rapidly. Traditional support systems are evolving, care costs are rising faster than general inflation, and new care options and funding solutions emerge regularly. Understanding these changes—and how to navigate them—is crucial for anyone who wants to protect themselves and their loved ones from the financial and emotional strain of unprepared long-term care needs.

As you read this book, you'll gain not just knowledge, but also the confidence to take action. Each chapter builds upon the previous ones, creating a comprehensive framework for understanding and addressing long-term care needs. From basic concepts to advanced planning strategies, from immediate concerns to long-term considerations, this guide will help you create a robust plan for whatever the future may bring.

The time to prepare for long-term care needs is now, before a crisis forces your hand. Let this book be your roadmap to understanding, planning for, and managing long-term care needs with confidence and clarity.

## Chapter 1: The New Reality of Long-Term Care

Let me share a story about Bob and Linda, a couple I met during one of my retirement planning workshops. They thought they had everything figured out. Both had worked for over 30 years, diligently saved in their 401(k)s, and were counting down the days to retirement. "We've done everything right," Bob told me, beaming with pride as he showed me their retirement portfolio. Their nest egg looked impressive—until we started talking about long-term care costs.

Like many Americans approaching retirement, Bob and Linda had built their retirement plan on what financial advisors traditionally called the three-legged stool: Social Security, pensions, and personal savings. On the surface, it seems like a solid framework. But here's the harsh reality: that stool is becoming increasingly wobbly, and for many, it's at risk of collapsing entirely.

## The First Leg: Social Security

Let's start with Social Security, the cornerstone of retirement income for millions of Americans. It was designed to provide a safety net, but cracks are starting to show. The Social Security Administration estimates that by 2034, the trust fund will only be able to pay about 77% of scheduled benefits unless significant changes are made. That's a potential 23% reduction in income for retirees who rely on it to cover basic needs like housing, groceries, and medical bills.

For Bob and Linda, a cut like this would force them to draw down their personal savings faster than planned—putting even more pressure on the third leg of their stool.

## The Second Leg: Pensions

The second leg, pensions, has been steadily disappearing. In the past, traditional pensions guaranteed a steady stream of income for retirees. But today, only about 15% of private-sector workers have access to a pension, down from nearly 88% in 1975. Instead, the shift to 401(k)s and IRAs has transferred the responsibility—and the risk—of retirement planning from employers to individuals.

Bob and Linda were fortunate enough to have employer-sponsored retirement accounts, but the burden of managing those savings, choosing investments, and making sure the money lasts throughout their retirement years was entirely on their shoulders.

## The Third Leg: Personal Savings

The third leg of the stool—personal savings—faces its own challenges. Even diligent savers like Bob and Linda can't ignore the growing threats of inflation, rising healthcare costs, and increased longevity. The numbers are staggering: according to Fidelity's 2024 Retiree Health Care Cost Estimate, a 65-year-old couple retiring today will need about $315,000 saved just to cover healthcare costs during retirement.

And that's before we even talk about long-term care. These costs are often a blind spot in retirement planning. Assisted living facilities, in-home caregivers, and nursing homes aren't cheap. A private room in a nursing home averages over $100,000 a year—and that number keeps climbing.

## The Medicare Misconception

A common misconception is that Medicare will step in and cover these costs. Unfortunately, that's not the case. Medicare doesn't pay for help with daily activities like bathing, dressing, or eating—the very types of assistance most people will eventually need. Skilled nursing care? Yes, but only under specific conditions and for a limited time.

This misunderstanding creates a dangerous gap in planning. Without a clear understanding of what Medicare covers—and more importantly, what it doesn't—many retirees are left unprepared for the realities of long-term care.

## Living Longer, Needing More

Thanks to advances in medicine, Americans are living longer than ever. While that's worth celebrating, it also comes with a catch: longer lives often mean more years needing care. According to the Department of Health and Human Services, someone turning 65 today has almost a 70% chance of needing some type of long-term care during their remaining years.

Now, add to that the "disappearing family caregiver" phenomenon. Families are smaller and more spread out geographically. Adult children, once the primary caregivers, are juggling their own careers and responsibilities. This leaves many retirees without the traditional safety net of family support.

## The Emotional and Financial Toll

The impact of long-term care isn't just financial; it's deeply emotional. Caregiving can place immense stress on family members, leading to burnout, strained relationships, and even health issues for the caregivers themselves. For retirees, the need for care can bring feelings of dependence, a loss of dignity, and anxiety about burdening loved ones.

**Maria's Story**

Maria's story is a sobering reminder of why planning for long-term care is so important. At 72, she thought she was financially secure. She had saved $800,000 over her career and felt confident in her retirement plan. But when her husband was diagnosed with Parkinson's disease, the costs of his care quickly mounted. In just five years, half of their savings were gone. "If I had known," Maria told me, tears in her eyes, "I would have planned differently."

## Common Myths About Long-Term Care

Many people overlook or delay planning for long-term care because of common misconceptions. Let's debunk a few:

**"Long-term care is only for the elderly."** In reality, anyone can need care at any age due to accidents or illnesses.

**"My family will take care of me."** While family support is invaluable, it may not be feasible given today's dispersed and busy lifestyles.

**"Medicare or Medicaid will cover everything."** Medicaid has strict eligibility requirements and often doesn't provide the quality or range of care many people expect.

## A New Approach to Retirement Planning

The new reality of long-term care requires a fresh approach to retirement planning. It's no longer enough to rely on Social Security, pensions, or even substantial savings. We need to factor in healthcare and long-term care costs as essential components of our plans, not as afterthoughts.

There are solutions. Strategies like long-term care insurance, hybrid policies, and asset protection planning can help mitigate the risks. Bob and Linda, for example, adjusted their strategy after learning about these options. By including long-term care planning in their overall retirement approach, they gained peace of mind and a renewed sense of security.

**Questions to Reflect On**

Before we move on, take a moment to consider your own situation:

Have you thought about how long-term care costs might affect your retirement savings?

Do you understand what Medicare covers and where the gaps are?

Have you discussed your preferences for care with your family?

**The Path Forward**

The challenges may seem daunting, but the good news is that you don't have to face them alone. With the right information, tools, and strategies, you can take control of your future and protect your family from the unexpected. Planning for long-term care isn't just about money—it's about peace of mind and ensuring the dignity and independence you deserve in retirement.

In the next chapter, we'll take a closer look at Medicare: what it covers, what it doesn't, and how to address the gaps. Understanding these details is the first step in creating a comprehensive plan for your future care needs.

## The Real Costs of Long-Term Care in 2025

When Janet called me last week, her voice trembled with worry. She had just received a quote for her mother's assisted living facility, and the numbers shocked her. "How can it possibly cost this much?" she asked. "And how do regular people manage to pay for it?" These are questions I hear almost daily, and they're exactly what we need to talk about.

Let's get real about the costs of long-term care in 2025. I won't sugarcoat it—the numbers can be intimidating. But understanding them is the first step toward creating a plan that works for you and your family.

**The True Costs of Care**

Let's start with home health aide services, since most people prefer to stay in their homes as long as possible. In 2025, the national average cost for a home health aide runs about $35 per hour. That might not sound too bad at first glance, but let's do the math together. If you need help for just four hours a day, five days a week, you're looking at about $3,000 monthly. Need full-time care? That jumps to nearly $7,300 per month.

Adult day care offers a more affordable option for families who need care during working hours. The national average sits at $85 per day in 2025. For many families, this provides a sweet spot—professional care and social interaction for their loved one during the day, while family members can provide care in the evenings and weekends. A month of adult day care, five days a week, averages around $1,800.

When we move into assisted living territory, the costs climb significantly. The national average for assisted living in 2025 runs about $5,200 per month. But here's something crucial to understand—that's just the base rate. Think of it like a cruise ship's basic fare. Just as you pay extra for shore excursions and specialty dining on a cruise, assisted living often has additional costs for services like medication management, special diets, or extra help with daily activities.
Now, let's talk about nursing homes, the most comprehensive care option available. In 2025, a semi-private room in a nursing home averages $8,900 per month nationally, while a private room tops $10,200. That's over $122,000 annually for a private room—more than many Americans earn in a year.

## Emotional and Financial Strain

For many families, the financial shock is only part of the story. The emotional toll of long-term care can be just as overwhelming. Janet shared how the rising costs made her feel trapped between wanting the best for her mother and maintaining her own financial stability. "It's heartbreaking," she said, "because I want to give her everything she needs, but I feel like I'm failing her."

This emotional burden underscores the importance of planning ahead. When families are prepared, they can focus on providing love and support instead of scrambling to manage the logistics.

**Regional and Inflationary Challenges**

These costs vary significantly by location. In some urban areas, expect to pay 30-40% more than the national average. In rural areas, you might pay less, but you'll have fewer options to choose from. For example, while a home health aide in Louisiana might cost $25 per hour, the same service in Massachusetts could run $40 or more. Assisted living in the Southeast might average $4,000 monthly, while the same level of care in the Northeast or West Coast could easily exceed $7,000.

Here's what makes this even more challenging: these costs are rising faster than general inflation. Over the past decade, long-term care costs have increased by an average of 3-4% annually, outpacing both general inflation and wage growth. This means that if you're planning for care needs ten years from now, you need to factor in significant cost increases.

**Planning for the Future**

Let me share a planning technique I use with my clients. Instead of focusing on today's costs, we project forward using a 4% annual increase. So if you're 55 now and think you might need care at 75, we need to plan for costs roughly double what they are today. That assisted living facility charging $5,200 per month now? In 20 years, it could cost over $11,000 per month.

## How Do People Pay for Long-Term Care?

Most families don't have the resources to absorb these costs out-of-pocket. According to AARP, nearly 45% of long-term care costs are paid directly by families, while Medicaid covers approximately 50% for those who qualify. However, Medicaid has strict eligibility requirements and often doesn't provide the level of care many people prefer. Long-term care insurance can be a solution for some, but only about 16% of Americans over 65 have such a policy. Other options include hybrid life insurance policies with long-term care riders, reverse mortgages, and creative care arrangements like shared housing or multi-generational living setups. Each of these approaches has pros and cons, and the right choice depends on your unique situation.

## A Practical Exercise

Take a moment to consider your family's potential needs. How many hours of care might you or a loved one require daily? Multiply that by the current hourly rate in your area to get a sense of monthly costs. Then, project those costs forward using a 4% annual increase. This exercise can give you a clearer picture of the financial challenges you may face and highlight the importance of starting to plan now.

## Balancing Challenges with Hope

While these numbers may seem daunting, the key is to take proactive steps. Throughout this book, we'll explore various strategies for managing these costs—from insurance solutions to innovative care arrangements. Remember, you wouldn't wait until retirement to start saving for it. Similarly, you shouldn't wait until you need care to figure out how to pay for it.

Think of it this way: planning ahead isn't just about money. It's about protecting your family from unnecessary stress, ensuring your dignity and independence, and making sure you receive the care you deserve. In the next chapter, we'll explore who typically needs long-term care and for how long, helping you better estimate your personal planning needs.

## The Hidden Costs of Long-Term Care

When most people think about long-term care costs, they focus on the big-ticket items\u2014the monthly fees for assisted living or the hourly rates for home health aides. But there's a whole world of hidden costs that can catch families off guard. I learned this lesson personally when helping my aunt age in place, and it's a story I now share with all my clients.

When my aunt first needed help, I assumed I could handle everything. Coordinating her appointments, managing medications, and ensuring her home was safe seemed straightforward enough. But three months in, I realized I was out of my depth. I hired a professional care coordinator for $150 an hour, and while it wasn't cheap, it was a game-changer. The care coordinator knew the healthcare system, had relationships with providers, and solved problems quickly. What felt like chaos to me was routine for them. That expertise was worth every penny.

Medical equipment is another hidden cost that can quickly add up. A hospital bed might cost anywhere from $500 to $3,000 depending on its features, and lifting equipment like a Hoyer lift can cost $5,000 or more. Then there are smaller but essential items\u2014shower chairs ($50-$200), grab bars ($20-$100 each), and wheelchair ramps ($1,000-$3,000). These costs accumulate fast, often before families even hire a caregiver.

Home modifications can be the most significant hidden expense. One client, Rachel, spent over $25,000 adapting her father's home so he could age in place. They widened doorways for wheelchair access, installed a walk-in shower, added grab bars throughout the house, and built a wheelchair ramp. While these changes were essential for her father's safety and independence, they hadn't been part of their initial budget. Stories like Rachel's highlight the importance of accounting for these costs early in the planning process.

Transportation is another overlooked expense. For seniors in areas without reliable public transit, door-to-door services become a necessity. Medical transport services, which often include assistance getting in and out of vehicles, cost $50-$100 per trip. For more specialized needs, like traveling to a specialist in another city, costs can easily reach several hundred dollars per trip. These expenses can be particularly burdensome for families managing multiple appointments each month.

Now let's address the elephant in the room: inflation. While general inflation hovers around 2-3% annually, long-term care costs have risen at a rate of 3-4% per year. To illustrate, a home health aide service costing $4,000 monthly today could rise to $7,800 by the time a 55-year-old needs care at age 75. These steady increases make it crucial to plan not just for today's costs but also for the future.

**A Hidden Costs Fund**

One strategy I recommend to clients is creating a "hidden costs fund." This is a separate savings account specifically for unexpected care-related expenses. By setting aside money now, you can avoid financial strain later and protect your other investments from being liquidated at inopportune times. While you might not need every dollar, having this buffer provides peace of mind.

**Resources to Offset Costs**

There are also resources available to help families manage hidden costs:

- **Local Nonprofits:** Many organizations offer grants for home modifications or provide medical equipment at reduced prices.
- **Government Programs:** Check for state or federal programs that offer subsidies for senior transportation or home accessibility improvements.
- **Tech Solutions:** Apps and online platforms like Care.com or AARP's Caregiving Resource Center can streamline care coordination and reduce stress.

**Plan with Confidence**

The goal of this section isn't to scare you but to prepare you. Understanding these hidden costs now allows you to incorporate them into your financial plan, reducing the risk of surprises down the road. In the next chapters, we'll explore specific strategies to address these costs, from insurance options to maximizing available resources. Remember, the key is to act now while you have the time and flexibility to make informed decisions.

## "It Won't Happen to Me"

"It won't happen to me." I hear this often in my workshops, usually from healthy, active people in their 50s and 60s. They exercise regularly, eat well, and have good genes on their side. Yet the statistics tell a different story—one that everyone approaching retirement needs to understand.

## Who Needs Long-Term Care?

Understanding Your Risk

Let's start with the numbers that often surprise people. According to the Department of Health and Human Services, someone turning 65 today has nearly a 70% chance of needing some type of long-term care services in their remaining years. For women, that probability rises to 75%. On average, people who need long-term care will require services for about three years. But these are just averages. Your personal risk profile is as unique as your fingerprint, shaped by various factors that we need to examine carefully.

## Current Statistics on Care Needs After 65

The probability of needing long-term care often comes as a shock. These numbers underscore the importance of preparation:

- Nearly 70% of individuals turning 65 today will need some type of long-term care.
- Women have a 75% likelihood of requiring care, compared to men.
- On average, people need care for about three years, but 20% will require it for more than five years.

## Key Risk Factors

### Family Health History

Family health history often provides our first clue about potential care needs. I recall working with twins, both in their mid-50s, whose mother had developed early-onset Alzheimer's. While having a parent with Alzheimer's doesn't guarantee you'll develop it, it does increase your risk. Understanding your family health patterns—from heart disease to diabetes to cognitive decline—helps you make more informed planning decisions. Have you considered your family's health history and how it might shape your future needs?

### Lifestyle Impacts

Lifestyle choices play a crucial role too, though perhaps not always in the ways you might expect. Yes, regular exercise, a healthy diet, and not smoking reduce your risk of needing care. But here's something that often surprises people: highly active individuals sometimes need more care in their later years because they live longer. Take my client Jack, a former marathon runner.

His healthy lifestyle helped him reach 92, but he needed assistance for the last five years of his life—longer than many of his less-active peers. This raises an interesting question: while living longer is a goal for many, have you planned for the years when assistance might be necessary?

**Gender Differences**

Gender differences in long-term care needs are striking. Women not only have a higher likelihood of needing care, but they often need it for longer periods—on average, 3.7 years compared to 2.2 years for men. This gender gap isn't just about longevity. Women are more likely to live alone in their later years and often have fewer financial resources due to career interruptions and historically lower wages. Have you factored in how these differences might affect your or your partner's future?

**Marital Status**

Marital status significantly impacts your long-term care risk profile. Married individuals generally need paid care for shorter periods than single people, partly because spouses often provide care for each other. However, this can create its own challenges. Sarah, a client in her 70s, spent three years caring for her husband after his stroke, only to find herself exhausted and facing her own health challenges afterward. Have you considered how caregiving responsibilities might affect both partners' well-being?

### Geographic Location

Geographic location affects both your risk of needing care and your access to care services. Urban areas typically offer more care options but at higher costs. Rural areas might have lower costs but fewer choices and longer distances to medical facilities. Climate plays a role too—areas with harsh winters can make it more challenging for older adults to maintain independence. Thinking about where you plan to age, have you assessed how the local environment might shape your care options?

### Common Health Triggers for Care

Common health triggers for care needs often develop gradually. The top three I see are cognitive decline, chronic conditions, and mobility issues. Alzheimer's and other forms of dementia are leading causes of long-term care needs. Chronic illnesses like diabetes, heart disease, or arthritis slowly erode independence, while mobility problems—often caused by falls—frequently signal the need for a transition to assisted care. Falls particularly concern me; they're the leading cause of fatal and non-fatal injuries for older Americans. One serious fall can instantly change your care needs. What steps have you taken to mitigate these risks in your home or lifestyle?

### Average Duration of Care Needs

Understanding average care durations helps with planning. While the average is three years, 20% of today's 65-year-olds will need care for more than five years. This variation makes planning challenging but even more essential. How would an extended care period affect your financial plans or family support system?

## Risk Assessment Tools and Calculators

This is why I encourage everyone to use risk assessment tools and calculators. The National Institute on Aging offers excellent resources for evaluating your personal risk factors. However, remember that these tools provide estimates based on current data—they can't predict individual outcomes with certainty. Have you used any of these tools to get a clearer picture of your potential needs?

## The "Alone Factor": Single vs. Married Risk Differences

Let's talk about what I call the "Alone Factor." Single people, whether never married, divorced, or widowed, face unique challenges. Without a spouse or partner to provide care, they typically need paid care services sooner and for longer periods. They also tend to need more comprehensive services when they do require care. If you're single, have you considered how you'll structure your support network for future care needs?

Your personal risk assessment should consider all these factors together. Someone with a family history of longevity, living in an area with limited care options, might need to plan differently than someone with a spouse, strong family support system, and easy access to care services.

As we move forward, we'll explore how to use this risk assessment to create a personalized care plan. Understanding your risk factors is just the first step—the real work comes in developing strategies to address them effectively.

## Types of Care – From Home Health to Nursing Facilities

Understanding the different types of long-term care options can feel like learning a new language. With so many terms and choices, it's easy to feel overwhelmed. Let's break these options down into simple, clear categories to help you or your loved ones make informed decisions. This chapter covers the spectrum of care, starting with home-based solutions and progressing to community and facility-based options.

## Home Care Options

For many people, the ideal scenario is to age in place, remaining in the comfort of their own homes for as long as possible. Home care options cater to varying levels of need, from basic assistance to skilled medical interventions.

- **Personal Care Assistants (PCAs):**
  Personal Care Assistants provide support with daily living activities such as bathing, dressing, grooming, meal preparation, and light housekeeping. They're often hired for their compassionate approach, helping individuals maintain their dignity and quality of life. PCAs are ideal for those who are still relatively independent but need extra support. For example, a PCA might visit for a few hours each day to assist with morning routines or meal prep, making a significant difference in both the individual's and their family's lives.

**Home Health Aides (HHAs):**

Home Health Aides take personal care a step further by incorporating health-related services. Trained and certified, HHAs monitor vital signs, assist with prescribed exercises, and even administer medication under the supervision of a healthcare professional. This blend of personal and medical care is crucial for individuals managing chronic conditions or recovering from illnesses.

- **Skilled Nursing Care:**
  Skilled nursing care at home brings the expertise of Registered Nurses (RNs) or Licensed Practical Nurses (LPNs) directly to individuals who need more intensive medical support. These professionals manage wound care, administer intravenous medications, monitor medical equipment, and address complex health issues. For someone recovering from surgery or managing a serious illness, skilled nursing care can provide peace of mind and a higher quality of life without the need to move to a facility.

- **Therapy Services:**
  Physical, occupational, and speech therapy services are also available in-home. These professionals help clients regain strength, mobility, and independence following surgery or injury. For instance, a physical therapist might work with a patient to rebuild strength after a hip replacement, while an occupational therapist focuses on strategies to perform daily tasks despite physical limitations. Speech therapists can assist those recovering from strokes to improve communication or swallowing difficulties.

## Community-Based Care

When staying at home is no longer sufficient but full-time facility care isn't yet necessary, community-based options can provide a middle ground.

- **Adult Day Care Centers:**
  These centers offer structured daytime care, giving family caregivers a much-needed break while ensuring their loved ones are well-cared for. Services often include meals, social activities, medication management, and health monitoring. Specialized programs, such as those for individuals with dementia, add an extra layer of tailored care.

- **Senior Centers:**
  Designed for active older adults, senior centers focus on social engagement, fitness classes, educational workshops, and wellness programs. While they do not provide personal care services, senior centers are an excellent resource for individuals looking to remain socially connected and active in their community.

- **PACE Programs (Program of All-Inclusive Care for the Elderly):**
  PACE programs combine comprehensive healthcare with supportive services, helping seniors who qualify for nursing home care to stay in their homes. Services are coordinated through a single organization and include medical care, therapy, transportation, and social activities. PACE programs simplify the logistics of care, providing an all-in-one solution for families.

## Assisted Living

For those needing more support than home or community-based care can provide, assisted living facilities offer a blend of independence and assistance.

- **Traditional Assisted Living:**
  These facilities provide private or semi-private apartments, along with services such as meals, housekeeping, and personal care assistance. They allow residents to maintain their autonomy while offering help as needed, making them a popular choice for individuals seeking a balance between independence and support.

- **Memory Care Units:**
  Tailored to individuals with Alzheimer's disease or other dementias, memory care units feature specialized staff, secure environments, and programs designed to enhance cognitive function and reduce confusion. These units are often part of larger assisted living facilities but may also stand alone.

- **Independent Living Plus:**
  Sometimes referred to as Enhanced Independent Living, these communities provide additional services like meal preparation, transportation, and wellness programs, catering to seniors who want independence with the added convenience of support.

- **Continuing Care Retirement Communities (CCRCs):**
  CCRCs offer a full continuum of care, allowing

residents to transition between independent living, assisted living, and skilled nursing care as their needs evolve. This all-in-one model provides stability and peace of mind, ensuring that care is available within the same community regardless of changes in health or mobility.

## Nursing Home Care

When medical needs become too complex for home or assisted living, nursing homes provide the highest level of care outside of hospitals.

- **Skilled Nursing Facilities (SNFs):**
  SNFs offer round-the-clock nursing care, making them a lifeline for individuals with significant medical needs. They cater to both short-term residents recovering from surgeries or illnesses and long-term residents requiring ongoing support.

- **Rehabilitation Services:**
  In addition to general care, nursing homes often provide intensive rehabilitation services for patients recovering from surgeries, strokes, or other debilitating conditions. Physical, occupational, and speech therapy are delivered more frequently and rigorously than in other settings.

- **Memory Care Units:**
  Within nursing homes, memory care units provide specialized care for residents with advanced cognitive decline. These units often feature secure facilities, individualized care plans, and staff

trained in managing challenging behaviors associated with dementia.

- **Specialty Care Units:**
  Beyond memory care, specialty units address unique medical needs such as ventilator care, bariatric care, or palliative services. These units cater to individuals requiring advanced medical technology or specialized attention.

## Adapting to Changing Needs

The journey through long-term care is rarely linear. Needs often evolve over time, requiring adjustments to the care plan. Understanding the various options allows families to make informed decisions and provide the best possible support for their loved ones.

In the next section, we'll explore a case study that demonstrates how a family successfully navigated these choices, ensuring their loved one received the right care at every stage.

## Hybrid Care Models: Redefining Long-Term Care

While traditional care options work well for many people, an exciting movement in long-term care is gaining momentum. These innovative approaches, often referred to as **hybrid care models**, combine the independence of aging in place with the security of readily available support services. These models emphasize community, mutual aid, and cost-effective solutions, challenging the conventional boundaries of elder care.

## The Village Model: A Concierge Community

One of the most inspiring examples of hybrid care is the Village model. This concept, which originated in Boston's Beacon Hill neighborhood, offers a grassroots approach to aging in place. Members pay an annual fee—typically between $400 and $800—to join their local Village organization. In return, they gain access to a network of vetted service providers, organized social activities, and volunteer assistance.

The Village model fosters a unique sense of community. Members can start as volunteers, assisting others with tasks like transportation, errands, or minor home repairs, and transition to receiving help themselves as their needs change. This reciprocity builds trust and strengthens bonds among members.

Here are some of the key features Villages often provide:

- **Transportation Assistance:** Members can request rides to medical appointments, grocery stores, or social events, often at a much lower cost than private services.

- **Home Maintenance Support:** Villages may connect members with volunteers or professionals for minor repairs, gardening, or snow removal.

- **Social Engagement:** From book clubs and group outings to fitness classes and movie nights, Villages organize activities that keep members connected and engaged.

- **Group Discounts:** Many Villages negotiate discounts for services like housekeeping, meal delivery, or wellness programs.

The Village model thrives on mutual support. For instance, Ellen, a member of her local Village in Boston, described it as "a concierge service and a community rolled into one." This innovative concept allows older adults to remain independent while staying active and engaged.

## Naturally Occurring Retirement Communities (NORCs)

Another fascinating hybrid model is the **Naturally Occurring Retirement Community (NORC)**. Unlike planned retirement developments, NORCs emerge organically when a large concentration of residents in a neighborhood, apartment complex, or community age in place together.

NORCs offer a compelling example of grassroots problem-solving. With the right support, they can evolve into vibrant hubs of senior-focused services. For example, Margaret's apartment complex became a NORC over 20 years as its residents aged together. Residents partnered with local healthcare providers and social service agencies to bring critical resources on-site, including:

- **Health Clinics:** Regular wellness checks and chronic disease management programs available within the community.

- **Exercise and Wellness Classes:** Activities like yoga, tai chi, and strength training tailored for older adults.

- **On-Site Social Services:** Weekly visits from social workers to provide support, counseling, and referrals.

The transformation of NORCs into supportive environments is often driven by residents' proactive efforts. These communities allow older adults to remain in familiar surroundings while benefiting from shared resources and services.

## Co-Housing: Intentional Communities for Aging

**Co-housing** represents a more intentional approach to hybrid care, blending independence with collaboration. This model involves small groups of people who live in close proximity, sharing resources and responsibilities while maintaining private living spaces.

Co-housing communities often feature:

- **Private Apartments and Shared Common Areas:** Residents have their own homes but come together in shared spaces for meals, events, or leisure activities.
- **Mutual Support Networks:** Neighbors assist each other with tasks like grocery shopping, transportation, or light caregiving.
- **Cost-Sharing:** Residents split the costs of services such as housekeeping, meal preparation, or maintenance.

Barbara and her friends are a great example of how informal co-housing can work. They purchased adjacent condominiums and created their own network of support, ensuring they could rely on one another for daily tasks and companionship.

Some co-housing communities intentionally incorporate an **intergenerational approach**, mixing older and younger residents. This dynamic creates natural opportunities for mutual support. Older adults might assist with childcare or mentoring, while younger neighbors provide help with technology or physical tasks. This arrangement benefits all participants, fostering a sense of belonging across generations.

## Benefits of Hybrid Models

The beauty of hybrid care models lies in their **flexibility and cost-effectiveness**. These options allow individuals to tailor their level of involvement and services to their specific needs. For example:

- Someone might begin by attending occasional social events at their local Village and later take advantage of transportation or in-home assistance as their needs increase.

- In co-housing communities, residents can adapt their mutual support networks to provide additional care as members age.

Cost is another significant advantage. While hybrid models may involve membership fees or shared expenses, they are typically far more affordable than traditional assisted living or full-time home care. Additionally, the focus on community and social engagement helps residents maintain their independence and well-being longer, delaying the need for more intensive care options.

### Considerations for Hybrid Models

While hybrid care models offer many benefits, they are not a one-size-fits-all solution. These models work best for individuals who:

- Value community connection and mutual support.
- Are relatively independent and capable of contributing to or organizing their care network.
- Have access to a local Village, NORC, or co-housing community—or are motivated to help create one.

It's also important to recognize that hybrid models require proactive involvement. Whether joining a Village or creating a co-housing arrangement, success depends on collaboration and commitment from participants.

## Exploring Local Options

If you're intrigued by hybrid care models, the first step is to research what's available in your area. Villages and NORCs are steadily growing in number, and co-housing communities are gaining popularity. Even if none exist nearby, the principles behind these models—mutual support, shared resources, and community connection—can inspire you to work with others in your community to develop similar solutions.

Hybrid care models represent a refreshing and innovative shift in how we think about aging. By prioritizing independence, community, and flexibility, they provide a meaningful alternative to traditional care options. Whether you join an established Village, collaborate with neighbors in a NORC, or create your own co-housing network, these models offer a path to aging with dignity, connection, and support.

**Case Study: The Johnson Family's Wake-Up Call**

The Johnson family's story illustrates how even the best-laid retirement plans can be upended by an unexpected health crisis. While David and Carol Johnson believed they were prepared for retirement, their experience highlights critical gaps in long-term care planning. This chapter explores their journey, the financial and emotional impact of their decisions, and the lessons others can learn to prepare for similar challenges.

**Initial Situation**

David and Carol Johnson epitomized a picture-perfect retirement. At ages 72 and 70, they had carefully built a stable financial foundation and enjoyed a comfortable lifestyle. David, a retired high school principal, and Carol, a former librarian, relished spending time with their two adult children and grandchildren. They had achieved significant financial milestones:

- **Retirement Savings:** $850,000 in IRAs and other accounts.
- **Debt-Free Home:** Valued at $400,000.
- **Monthly Income:** Combined Social Security benefits of $4,200 and David's $3,000 pension.
- **Emergency Fund:** $50,000 in liquid savings.

Their health was manageable, with David controlling high blood pressure and mild arthritis, and Carol addressing early-stage osteoporosis through yoga and regular exercise. Their support system seemed strong, with one child, Sarah, living nearby, and the other, Michael, maintaining close contact from across the country. They had even taken proactive steps like installing grab bars in their bathrooms after Carol's minor fall.

Despite their preparation, they had overlooked crucial aspects of long-term care planning, which became evident when an unforeseen crisis struck.

**The Triggering Event**

The Johnsons' lives changed drastically when David suffered a major stroke while gardening. The stroke left him with partial paralysis on his right side, significant cognitive impairment, and speech difficulties. The immediate response was swift, thanks to Sarah, who happened to stop by that morning, but the stroke's effects created a cascade of challenges for the family.

After two weeks in the hospital, the medical team recommended intensive rehabilitation. Medicare initially covered David's stay in a skilled nursing facility, but coverage was limited to 100 days, contingent on ongoing improvement. This presented the family with their first difficult decision: should they opt for inpatient rehabilitation or coordinate care at home?

The stroke's impact rippled through the family:

- **Sarah's Role:** As the local child, Sarah took on the primary caregiving role, balancing her teaching job, her own family responsibilities, and managing her father's care.

- **Michael's Guilt:** Living across the country, Michael struggled with feelings of helplessness and made multiple trips to assist temporarily.

- **Carol's Overwhelm:** Carol, unaccustomed to handling finances and logistical decisions, became overwhelmed by medical bills, insurance paperwork, and the stress of daily visits to David's rehabilitation facility.

**Financial Impact**
The financial burden became apparent almost immediately. Although Medicare provided initial coverage, the Johnsons quickly encountered out-of-pocket costs that strained their savings. Within the first month, they incurred:

- **Medical Expenses:**
  - $3,200 in copayments and deductibles.
  - $2,800 for medical equipment, including a wheelchair and specialized bed.
  - $1,500 for additional home modifications, such as widening doorways and installing ramps.
- **Ongoing Care Costs:**
  - Home health aide (8 hours/day): $4,800 monthly.
  - Physical therapy (2 sessions/week): $400 monthly.
  - Occupational therapy: $350 monthly.
  - Speech therapy: $300 monthly.

Over the first year, the Johnsons spent nearly $100,000 of their retirement savings. The emergency fund was depleted within four months, forcing Carol to dip into their IRA accounts, which triggered additional taxes. The sudden financial strain left Carol questioning her own financial security, especially given her family history of Alzheimer's disease.

The emotional toll was equally significant. Sarah reduced her teaching hours, impacting her household income, while Carol's health began to deteriorate under the stress. Family tensions arose as Michael and Sarah disagreed on care decisions, highlighting the need for clear communication and advance planning.

**Lessons Learned**

The Johnsons' experience underscores critical areas where better preparation could have eased their financial and emotional burdens. Here's what we can learn from their story:

**What They Did Right**

- **Maintained an Emergency Fund:** The $50,000 in savings provided immediate financial relief, although it was quickly depleted.
- **Debt-Free Living:** Owning their home outright prevented additional financial strain from mortgage payments.
- **Proactive Home Modifications:** Small changes, like grab bars, helped make the home safer, though more extensive modifications were needed later.
- **Strong Relationships:** Their close family ties provided emotional and practical support during the crisis.
- **Detailed Records:** David's organization of medical and financial documents saved valuable time during the initial stages of planning.

**Missed Opportunities**

1. **Long-Term Care Insurance and Annuities:** While the Johnsons briefly considered traditional use it or lose it long-term care insurance in their 60s, they dismissed it as too expensive. However, they overlooked **Long-Term Care (LTC) Annuities**, which could have provided a more cost-effective and flexible solution. Unlike traditional insurance, LTC annuities offer a dual benefit: they grow as a retirement asset and provide enhanced payouts for long-term care expenses when needed. For example, the funds in an LTC annuity could have covered the home health aide costs and therapy expenses, significantly reducing the financial strain on their retirement savings. This option would have allowed them to allocate a portion of their existing assets into a tax-advantaged vehicle that grows while protecting against future care costs.

2. **Power of Attorney and Healthcare Directives:** The Johnsons had basic documents in place, but they hadn't updated them in years. This outdated paperwork caused confusion and delays during critical moments. An updated **Durable Power of Attorney** would have ensured a seamless transition of financial decision-making to Carol or their children. Similarly, a clearly outlined healthcare directive could have empowered their family to make informed care decisions without unnecessary stress or conflict.

3. **Asset Organization:**
   David had always managed the family's finances, leaving Carol unprepared to take over in an emergency. Without a clear, comprehensive overview of their accounts, insurance policies, and financial obligations, Carol struggled to locate critical information. Organizing their assets in advance—perhaps with the help of a financial advisor—could have eased this burden and allowed for quicker access to the resources needed during the crisis.

4. **Care Preferences:**
   The Johnsons had never discussed their long-term care preferences in depth with their children, leaving Michael and Sarah to navigate care decisions without clear guidance. This lack of communication led to disagreements, particularly about whether David should return home or receive care in a facility. Explicitly outlining care preferences in advance would have minimized these conflicts and provided clarity during an emotionally charged time.

## Why LTC Annuities Are a Better Option

Long-term care annuities offer several advantages over traditional LTC insurance or relying solely on savings:

- **Guaranteed Benefits:** Unlike traditional LTC insurance, LTC annuities don't involve the risk of "use-it-or-lose-it." If care isn't needed, the annuity remains a financial asset, providing growth or a death benefit for heirs.

- **Tax Advantages:** LTC annuities often come with tax-deferred growth and tax-free withdrawals when used for qualifying long-term care expenses, making them an efficient financial planning tool.

- **Simplified Underwriting:** LTC annuities generally have more lenient health requirements compared to traditional LTC insurance, making them accessible even for individuals with pre-existing conditions.

- **Flexible Payouts:** These annuities can provide enhanced payouts during long-term care periods, ensuring that funds are available precisely when they are needed most.

In the Johnsons' case, redirecting a portion of their retirement savings into an LTC annuity could have protected their financial stability and ensured the care David required without depleting their assets.

By incorporating solutions like LTC annuities into a comprehensive financial plan, families can create a safety net that addresses both immediate and future care needs, providing peace of mind and long-term financial security.

**Action Steps for Readers**

The Johnsons' experience offers valuable lessons for anyone planning for long-term care. Consider these action steps:

**Immediate Actions (Next 30 Days):**

- Organize all financial, medical, and insurance documents.

- Update legal documents (power of attorney, healthcare directives, wills).

- List all medications, doctors, and medical history.
- Discuss care preferences with family members.
- Research local care providers and long-term care options.

**Short-Term Planning (3–6 Months):**

- Evaluate long-term care insurance or alternative funding strategies.
- Create an inventory of assets and accounts.
- Develop a communication plan for family members to address caregiving roles.
- Research home modification options and costs.
- Identify local respite care services.

**Long-Term Strategies:**

- Conduct annual reviews of legal and financial documents.
- Hold regular family meetings to reassess care preferences and plans.
- Explore hybrid care models (e.g., Villages or NORCs) to build community support.
- Prioritize self-care for caregivers to prevent burnout.
- Plan for transitions, including potential facility-based care.

**Final Thoughts**

The Johnson family's story is a cautionary tale and a source of inspiration. While David never fully recovered his independence, the family learned to adapt. Carol embraced her new role managing their finances, Sarah found a balance between caregiving and her own family, and Michael's extended visits provided much-needed respite.

As Carol reflected, "We thought we were prepared for retirement, but we weren't prepared for this. If sharing our story helps others plan better, then it's worth it."

Long-term care planning isn't about predicting every scenario. It's about creating a flexible framework that can adapt to life's uncertainties. The Johnsons' experience highlights the importance of proactive planning, open communication, and the strength of family support when facing life's unexpected challenges.

## Chapter 2: What Medicare Actually Covers

"But I thought Medicare would cover that." This phrase is a common refrain in my practice, often uttered by families facing their first significant long-term care expense. The widespread confusion surrounding Medicare coverage is one of the greatest obstacles to effective long-term care planning. Let's clear up the misconceptions and examine precisely what Medicare does—and doesn't—cover when it comes to long-term care.

This expanded chapter delves deeply into the nuances of Medicare's coverage, providing actionable insights and strategies to navigate the system and plan effectively for care needs.

## Medicare's Long-Term Care Gap

The fundamental concept to grasp is the distinction between **skilled care** and **custodial care**. While these terms may sound technical, they are critical to understanding Medicare's limitations.

- **Skilled Care:** This refers to medical or rehabilitative services provided by licensed professionals such as nurses, physical therapists, or occupational therapists. Examples include wound care, intravenous medication administration, or post-surgical rehabilitation. Medicare typically covers skilled care under certain conditions.

- **Custodial Care:** This involves non-medical assistance with basic daily activities such as bathing, dressing, eating, and using the bathroom. While essential for many seniors, custodial care is generally not covered by Medicare unless provided in conjunction with skilled care.

## The Real-World Implications

Consider the case of Ruth, a client who suffered a stroke. Medicare covered her hospital stay and the initial skilled rehabilitation services she needed. But once Ruth was stable enough to leave the rehabilitation facility, Medicare stopped paying for her care, even though she still needed assistance with bathing, dressing, and meal preparation. Her family was shocked to learn that custodial care would have to be paid out of pocket.

This distinction between skilled and custodial care creates a substantial gap in Medicare coverage, leaving families responsible for significant expenses.

## Coverage Limitations Beyond Type of Care

Even within the realm of skilled care, Medicare imposes strict limitations, including:

1. **Time Restrictions:** Coverage for skilled nursing facility (SNF) care is limited to 100 days per benefit period, with significant copayments after day 20.

2. **Qualifying Conditions:** A three-day inpatient hospital stay is required before Medicare will cover SNF care.

3. **Location Requirements:** Care must be provided

in Medicare-certified facilities or by certified home health agencies.

### The Financial Impact

The costs of long-term care not covered by Medicare can be staggering:

- **Home Health Aide Services:** $4,300 per month (2025 average).
- **Nursing Home Care:** $9,000 or more per month for a private room.

Studies estimate that the average person turning 65 today will incur $120,000 in out-of-pocket long-term care costs. These figures highlight the importance of planning ahead to address the gaps in Medicare coverage.

## Part A Coverage Limitations

### The Three-Day Rule

Medicare Part A requires a three-day hospital stay as an admitted patient before covering skilled nursing facility care. However, if you are under "observation status" in the hospital—an increasingly common designation—this rule isn't met, and subsequent SNF care is not covered.

Take my client James, for example. After a four-day hospital stay following a fall, James was denied Medicare coverage for SNF care because he was classified under observation status rather than admitted as an inpatient. His family had to pay $12,000 out of pocket for his rehabilitation.

## SNF Coverage Details

Once qualified, Medicare provides tiered coverage for SNF care:

- **Days 1-20:** Medicare pays 100% of covered costs.
- **Days 21-100:** The patient pays a daily copayment ($204 in 2025).
- **Beyond Day 100:** The patient pays all costs.

Additional requirements for SNF coverage include:

- A doctor's certification of the need for skilled care.
- The facility must be Medicare-certified.
- The care must be provided daily and require the expertise of skilled professionals.

## Home Health Care Restrictions

Medicare Part A also covers limited home health services, but the eligibility criteria are strict:

- You must be considered **homebound**, meaning leaving home requires significant effort.
- The care must involve intermittent skilled nursing or therapy services.
- A physician must certify the need for home health services.

Even when Medicare covers home health care, it does not cover custodial care or 24-hour care.

## The 100-Day Rule Explained

The 100-day rule is one of the most misunderstood features of Medicare. A **benefit period** begins when you are admitted to a hospital as an inpatient and ends when you have not received any hospital or SNF care for 60 consecutive days. Within each benefit period, Medicare covers up to 100 days of SNF care.

## How Benefit Periods Work

Consider Patricia's story. She had a hip replacement in January, followed by a three-day hospital stay. Medicare covered her rehabilitation in an SNF for 45 days. Later that year, she suffered a stroke and required another SNF stay. Since more than 60 days had passed between her discharges, this counted as a new benefit period, and her SNF coverage reset to 100 days.

Key points to remember:

- Benefit periods do not automatically reset annually—they depend on the timing of hospital or SNF care.
- If you require additional SNF care within 60 days of discharge, you are still in the same benefit period.

## Pitfalls of the 100-Day Rule

Families often encounter issues related to:

1. **Breaks in Care:** If a patient returns home and then needs to go back to an SNF within 60 days, the remaining days in the current benefit period apply.
2. **Transfers:** Moving between SNFs must be

handled carefully to maintain Medicare coverage. Proper documentation of the need for skilled care is critical.

## Importance of Documentation

Medicare coverage hinges on thorough medical documentation, including:

- Detailed admission records.
- Daily nursing and therapy progress notes.
- Regular certifications of the need for skilled care.
- Clear evidence of progress or maintenance goals.

Without adequate documentation, Medicare may deny coverage, leaving families responsible for significant expenses.

## Supplementing Medicare Coverage

Medicare's limitations make it essential to explore supplemental insurance options and other strategies to fill the gaps. These options can protect against the financial strain of long-term care costs.

## Medicare Supplement (Medigap) Plans

Medigap policies are designed to cover some of the out-of-pocket costs not covered by Original Medicare, such as copayments, coinsurance, and deductibles. However, Medigap plans generally do not cover long-term custodial care or services like home health aides.

## Medicare Advantage Plans

While Medicare Advantage plans often include additional benefits, such as dental, vision, and wellness programs, they also have limitations. Coverage for long-term care remains minimal, and many plans impose narrow provider networks and strict authorization requirements.

## Long-Term Care Annuities

**Long-term care annuities** are a financial tool that can provide dual benefits:

1. **Asset Growth:** Funds in the annuity grow tax-deferred.

2. **Enhanced Payouts for Care:** When care is needed, the annuity provides higher payouts specifically for long-term care expenses.

Unlike traditional long-term care insurance, LTC annuities do not operate on a "use-it-or-lose-it" basis. If care is never required, the remaining balance can be left to heirs. Additionally, LTC annuities often feature more lenient underwriting, making them accessible to individuals with pre-existing conditions.

## Standalone Long-Term Care Insurance

Traditional long-term care insurance remains a viable option for some families, particularly when purchased at a younger age. Policies can cover custodial care, home health aides, and nursing home care. However, the rising cost of premiums and strict underwriting standards can make this option less appealing.

## Planning Ahead: Actionable Steps

To avoid the financial and emotional strain of Medicare's limitations, consider the following steps:

**Immediate Actions**

1. Educate yourself and your family about Medicare's rules and limitations.
2. Review your current Medicare plan to understand its coverage and exclusions.
3. Organize financial and medical documents to ensure accessibility during emergencies.

**Mid-Term Planning**

1. Explore supplemental coverage options, such as Medigap, LTC insurance, or LTC annuities.
2. Evaluate potential long-term care needs and associated costs in your area.
3. Begin discussions with family members about care preferences and financial responsibilities.

**Long-Term Strategies**

1. Periodically review and update your care plan, including any supplemental insurance policies.
2. Make home modifications early to support aging in place.
3. Regularly assess your financial readiness for long-term care expenses, adjusting your plan as needed.

## Supplemental Insurance Options

Now that we understand Medicare's limitations, let's delve deeper into how to fill those gaps effectively. Supplemental insurance can offer critical financial protection, but navigating the available options can feel overwhelming. My client David once asked, "There are so many options—how do I know which one is right for me?" The answer lies in understanding how each type of coverage works, its limitations, and how it fits your unique needs.

## Medigap Plans

Medigap plans, also known as Medicare Supplement Insurance, are specifically designed to help cover the out-of-pocket costs associated with Original Medicare. These include deductibles, copayments, and coinsurance. Think of Medigap as your financial safety net, stepping in when Medicare falls short.

**Key Features**

1. **Coverage for Skilled Nursing Facility Costs:** Certain Medigap plans, such as Plan G and Plan N, provide coverage for the copayments associated with skilled nursing facility (SNF) care. This is especially valuable during days 21-100 of a benefit period when Medicare requires a daily copayment (projected at $204 per day in 2025). Without Medigap, these costs could amount to over $16,000 for an extended SNF stay.

2. **Foreign Travel Emergency Coverage:** Some plans include benefits for emergency healthcare services abroad, offering peace of mind

for retirees who enjoy travel.

3. **Predictable Costs:** Medigap plans offer the advantage of predictable monthly premiums, making it easier to budget for healthcare expenses.

**Limitations**

- Medigap plans do **not** cover custodial care, prescription drugs, or services outside the scope of Original Medicare.
- They also won't extend Medicare's 100-day limit for SNF care.

**Cost Considerations**

Medigap premiums vary by location, age, and plan. In 2025, premiums typically range from $150 to $400 per month. While this might seem expensive, the savings can be substantial. For example, my client Margaret paid $2,400 annually for her Plan G but saved over $12,000 in SNF copayments after her hip replacement.

## Medicare Advantage Plans

Medicare Advantage plans, offered by private insurance companies, are an alternative to Original Medicare. These plans replace your Medicare Part A and Part B coverage and often include additional benefits.

**Key Features**

1. **Additional Services:** Many Medicare Advantage plans now offer benefits that Original Medicare doesn't, such as

coverage for personal care services, transportation to medical appointments, and meal delivery after hospital stays. Some even include limited short-term home care benefits.

2. **Lower Premiums:** Medicare Advantage plans often have lower monthly premiums than Medigap plans—some plans even offer $0 premiums.

3. **Integrated Coverage:** Plans often include prescription drug coverage (Part D), reducing the need for a separate policy.

**Limitations**

- **Network Restrictions:** Most Medicare Advantage plans require you to use network providers, which can limit your choices of doctors, hospitals, and SNFs. My client Robert experienced this firsthand when the nearest in-network SNF was 45 minutes away.

- **Cost Structure:** While monthly premiums may be low, out-of-pocket costs for copayments and coinsurance can add up quickly, especially if extensive care is needed. In 2025, the average out-of-pocket maximum for Medicare Advantage plans is $8,300.

## Other Insurance Options

Supplemental coverage beyond Medigap and Medicare Advantage can provide targeted financial protection.

**Hospital Indemnity Plans**

- **What They Cover:** These plans pay a fixed daily

benefit for hospital stays, regardless of other insurance coverage.

- **Cost:** Monthly premiums range from $25 to $100. Daily benefits are typically $100-$400 per day of hospitalization.

- **Best Use:** These plans can help cover deductibles, copayments, or additional expenses during a hospital stay.

### Critical Illness Insurance

- **What They Cover:** A lump sum payment if you're diagnosed with a covered condition, such as a heart attack, stroke, or cancer.

- **Cost:** A 65-year-old might pay $100-$150 per month for a $20,000 benefit.

- **Best Use:** Provides financial flexibility for both medical and non-medical expenses during a health crisis.

### Short-Term Care Insurance

- **What They Cover:** Up to one year of coverage for nursing home, assisted living, or home care services.

- **Cost:** Premiums are typically $100-$200 per month at age 65, with daily benefits ranging from $150 to $200.

- **Best Use:** Easier to qualify for than traditional long-term care insurance and a good option for bridging short-term care gaps.

**Long-Term Care Annuities**

- **What They Cover:** LTC annuities provide enhanced payouts specifically for long-term care expenses while offering tax-deferred growth on the investment.

- **Key Advantage:** If care isn't needed, the annuity balance remains part of your estate and can be passed to heirs.

- **Cost:** The initial investment varies but often starts at $50,000. These annuities are particularly useful for individuals who want to protect their assets while maintaining flexibility.

**Coverage Coordination**

Effectively using supplemental insurance requires understanding how these options interact and ensuring seamless coordination.

**Medicare as the Primary Payer**

Medicare pays first for covered services. Your supplemental insurance—whether Medigap, Medicare Advantage, or another policy—kicks in as the secondary payer.

**Avoiding Authorization Pitfalls**

Each type of insurance may have its own authorization requirements, and failing to meet them can result in denied claims. For instance:

- Medicare Advantage plans often require pre-authorization for certain services, even if Medicare itself doesn't.

- Hospital indemnity plans may require detailed hospital records to verify eligibility for payouts.

## Appealing Denied Claims

When claims are denied, you have the right to appeal. Each type of insurance has its own appeal process, and beneficiaries who persist often succeed. For example, about 80% of Medicare appeals result in a favorable outcome when pursued fully.

## Tailoring Your Coverage to Your Needs

The right combination of supplemental insurance depends on your unique circumstances. Consider these factors when evaluating your options:

1. **Health Status and Family History:** If you have a family history of conditions requiring long-term care, options like LTC annuities or short-term care insurance may be prudent.

2. **Financial Resources:** Evaluate your ability to afford premiums and balance them against potential out-of-pocket expenses.

3. **Healthcare Preferences:** Do you prefer the flexibility of choosing any Medicare provider (Medigap) or the additional benefits offered by Medicare Advantage?

4. **Anticipated Needs:** Assess the likelihood of needing services like SNF care, home health aides, or personal care.

## Real-World Example

David, the client mentioned earlier, carefully evaluated his options. He ultimately chose a Medigap Plan G for its flexibility, as he wanted access to any Medicare provider without worrying about network restrictions. Additionally, he invested in a long-term care annuity to protect against custodial care expenses. This combination provided him with peace of mind, predictable costs, and financial security.

**Conclusion**

Supplemental insurance options can bridge critical gaps in Medicare coverage, but choosing the right combination requires careful consideration. Whether it's Medigap, Medicare Advantage, or additional coverage like LTC annuities, each option serves a specific purpose. By understanding how these plans work together and aligning them with your personal needs, you can build a comprehensive safety net that protects your finances and ensures access to quality care.

**Case Study 1: The Coverage Gap Surprise (Expanded)**

Richard and Elena Martinez believed they had done everything right. With successful careers behind them—Richard as an engineer and Elena as a high school teacher—they entered retirement confident in their financial preparation and healthcare choices. However, their story illustrates how even well-prepared families can be blindsided by Medicare's limitations. It's a cautionary tale about the importance of understanding coverage gaps and planning for the unexpected.

**Family Situation**

The Martinezes were a typical middle-class couple enjoying their retirement. At ages 68 and 66, they had carefully managed their finances and were in a relatively strong position:

- **Retirement Savings:** $600,000 in a mix of IRAs and taxable accounts.
- **Monthly Income:** $4,200 from combined Social Security benefits and $2,000 from Elena's modest pension as a retired teacher.
- **Home Equity:** Their home was valued at $350,000, with a small remaining mortgage.
- **Health:** Both were generally healthy. Richard managed high blood pressure with medication, and Elena controlled arthritis pain with prescribed treatments.
- **Support System:** Two adult children living within driving distance, who were available to assist when needed.

Despite their preparations, the couple made one significant misstep—they opted for **Original Medicare without supplemental coverage**. They believed their good health and disciplined financial habits would minimize their need for additional insurance, allowing them to avoid higher monthly premiums. Unfortunately, this decision left them exposed to significant out-of-pocket costs when Richard suffered a sudden health crisis.

**The Triggering Event**
The event that changed everything began as a typical morning. Richard was working in the garden when he suddenly collapsed. Elena found him and called 911, and he was rushed to the hospital, where doctors diagnosed a stroke. After five days of inpatient care, the medical team recommended transferring Richard to a skilled nursing facility (SNF) for intensive rehabilitation.

Initially, everything went smoothly. Medicare covered the costs for the first 20 days of Richard's SNF stay. He was making progress, and the couple felt relieved that his care seemed manageable. However, on **day 21**, they received their first bill—$200 per day in copayments. They were shocked to learn that Medicare required these payments for days 21-100 in a skilled nursing facility, a detail they had completely misunderstood.
Richard's recovery was slower than expected, and his doctors recommended a 60-day stay. The Martinezes faced a harsh reality: they would owe $8,000 for the next 40 days of care. This financial blow was just the beginning.

**Planning Oversights**
The Martinezes' experience revealed several critical oversights in their retirement and healthcare planning:

1. **Misunderstanding Medicare's Skilled Nursing Coverage:**
   They hadn't realized that Medicare's SNF coverage includes **significant copayments starting on day 21**, nor that these costs could escalate quickly during an extended stay.

2. **Lack of Supplemental Coverage:**
   By opting out of a Medigap plan, they left themselves responsible for covering the

substantial gaps in Medicare coverage.

3. **Insufficient Emergency Fund:** While they had retirement savings, they didn't maintain a dedicated healthcare emergency fund for unexpected costs.

4. **Limited Family Discussions:** They hadn't discussed with their children how they would handle extended care needs or who would manage logistical challenges if one parent faced a health crisis.

5. **No Medicare Specialist Consultation:** They didn't seek professional advice before choosing their Medicare coverage, leaving them unaware of the program's limitations.

**Financial Consequences**

The financial impact of Richard's stroke was severe:

- **Skilled Nursing Facility Copayments:** $16,000 for 40 days at $200 per day.

- **Uncovered Medical Equipment and Supplies:** $3,000 for a wheelchair, walker, and additional aids not covered by Medicare.

- **Transportation Costs:** $2,500 for follow-up medical appointments and therapy sessions, including specialized transport services.

- **Home Modifications:** $5,000 for installing grab bars, a ramp, and widening doorways to accommodate Richard's wheelchair.

To cover these unexpected expenses, the Martinezes had to:

- Withdraw funds from their retirement accounts, triggering **tax liabilities** that further depleted their savings.
- Use credit cards for some expenses, incurring high interest charges.
- Accept financial assistance from their children, creating stress and straining family relationships.

**Proper Planning Steps**

The Martinezes' experience taught them valuable lessons about the importance of proactive planning. With the help of a Medicare specialist, they took several key steps to protect themselves from future healthcare surprises:

1. **Enrolling in a Medigap Plan G:**
   This plan now covers their skilled nursing facility copayments, providing financial protection if Richard requires another SNF stay.

2. **Creating a Dedicated Healthcare Emergency Fund:**
   They set aside $25,000 specifically for unexpected medical expenses, ensuring they wouldn't need to rely on credit cards or retirement withdrawals in the future.

3. **Developing a Family Care Coordination Plan:**
   They worked with their children to establish clear roles and responsibilities, including how to handle emergencies, manage care logistics, and share financial burdens.

4. **Maintaining Better Documentation:** They began keeping detailed records of all medical care, bills, and insurance correspondence to avoid confusion and facilitate reimbursement claims.

5. **Regular Medicare Reviews:** They committed to an annual review of their Medicare coverage with a specialist to ensure their plan continues to meet their needs.

**Action Steps for Readers**

The Martinez family's experience provides a clear roadmap for avoiding similar pitfalls. Here are the actionable steps every Medicare beneficiary should take:

**Documentation Requirements**

- Keep a detailed medical history, including hospital stays and treatments.
- Save all Medicare notices, bills, and insurance statements.
- Maintain a log of conversations with healthcare providers and insurance representatives, including dates and key points discussed.
- Document all medications, dosages, and prescribing doctors.

**Essential Questions to Ask**

- What is my status (inpatient vs. observation) during hospital stays?
- Is this facility Medicare-certified?
- What services are included in the daily rate?

- What are the expected out-of-pocket costs for my care?
- What is my expected length of stay, and will Medicare continue coverage throughout?

**Appeal Procedures**

- Understand your rights to appeal Medicare decisions.
- Keep copies of all denial notices and supporting documentation.
- Follow appeal deadlines precisely.
- Gather letters from healthcare providers to support your case.
- Seek professional assistance for complex appeals.

**Professional Help Guidelines**

- Consult a Medicare specialist to review your plan options before enrolling.
- Work with a financial advisor to incorporate healthcare costs into your retirement plan.
- Consider consulting an elder law attorney for estate and long-term care planning.
- Use free resources like your State Health Insurance Assistance Program (SHIP) for guidance.

**Lessons Learned**

The Martinez family's story highlights the importance of understanding Medicare's coverage gaps and taking proactive steps to address them. As Elena now tells her friends, "Don't assume Medicare will cover everything. Ask questions, get professional help, and plan for the unexpected. What you don't know really can hurt you financially."

Their case underscores a vital truth: Medicare coverage gaps can surprise even the most prepared families. By learning from their experience and taking action now, you can avoid costly mistakes and ensure you're ready to face any challenges that arise.

**Medicare Conclusion**

Understanding what Medicare does and doesn't cover is a critical step in planning for long-term care. While Medicare provides essential coverage for skilled care, its limitations on custodial care and other services leave many families financially vulnerable. By supplementing Medicare with additional coverage options, such as LTC annuities or standalone policies, you can bridge the gaps and ensure financial stability.

The key takeaway is that proactive planning makes all the difference. With the right strategies in place, you can navigate the complexities of Medicare and long-term care with confidence, protecting both your finances and your peace of mind.

# Chapter 3: How to Pay for Long-Term Care

## Traditional Long-Term Care Insurance

When Susan visited my office, she carried a stack of brochures nearly six inches high and sighed, "I've been reading these for weeks, and I'm more confused now than when I started." Susan's experience is not uncommon. Traditional long-term care insurance (LTCI) can feel overwhelming due to the variety of options, terminology, and complex considerations involved. Let's simplify the discussion by breaking down the essential components of LTCI, how it works, and why it might be the right choice for some.

## Policy Types and Features

At its core, LTCI is a financial safety net designed specifically for long-term care needs. It pays for care when you can no longer independently perform daily activities like bathing, dressing, or eating. Policies come in several types, each tailored to different needs and budgets:

1. **Comprehensive Policies:** These are the most popular and flexible type of LTCI. Comprehensive policies cover care across multiple settings, including:
    - In-home care
    - Adult day care centers
    - Assisted living facilities

- Nursing homes

This flexibility allows policyholders to receive care where they feel most comfortable, making comprehensive policies a preferred choice for those who want to age in place.

2. **Facility-Only Policies:** These policies limit coverage to care provided in licensed facilities, such as nursing homes or assisted living communities. While they're generally less expensive than comprehensive policies, their lack of flexibility can be a drawback. For individuals with tight budgets, however, these policies can still provide critical protection against catastrophic care costs.

3. **Shared Care Policies:** Couples can benefit from shared care policies, which pool their benefits into a single pot. For example, if each partner purchases a policy with three years of coverage, they collectively have six years of coverage that either partner can use. This option provides peace of mind and financial efficiency, especially if one partner requires significantly more care than the other.

**Key Coverage Elements**

Understanding the foundational elements of LTCI policies is essential to selecting the right one. Every policy includes four critical components:

1. **Daily or Monthly Benefit Amount:** This is the maximum amount the policy will pay for care. In 2025, $200 daily or $6,000 monthly is a typical recommendation to cover average care costs. However, the appropriate amount may vary depending on local care costs and personal circumstances.

2. **Benefit Period:** The length of time the policy will pay for care is called the benefit period. Options usually range from two years to lifetime coverage. Since the average need for long-term care lasts about three years, many people choose this as a starting point, although longer periods provide more security.

3. **Elimination Period:** This is the waiting period before benefits kick in, measured in days rather than dollars. Common elimination periods are 30, 60, or 90 days. During this time, you are responsible for paying for care out of pocket. A longer elimination period can lower your premiums but requires careful planning to ensure funds are available to cover the gap.

4. **Inflation Protection:** One of the most crucial features for younger buyers, inflation protection ensures that your benefits keep pace with rising care costs. For example, a 3% compound inflation option

increases your benefits by 3% annually, providing significantly more coverage as time goes on. Without this feature, a policy purchased at age 55 may cover only half of the actual costs by the time you need care.

## Premium Stability and Industry Trends

One major concern for LTCI buyers is the potential for premium increases. In the early days of LTCI, insurers underestimated how many policyholders would retain their coverage and the costs of long-term care claims, leading to significant premium hikes for many early adopters. While today's policies are priced more accurately, it's still important to understand the factors influencing premium stability:

- **Interest Rates:** Insurers rely on investment returns to keep premiums stable. Prolonged periods of low interest rates can create financial pressures, leading to rate increases.

- **Claims Experience:** Higher-than-expected claims, such as an increase in people needing care or using their benefits longer than anticipated, can impact premiums.

- **Policyholder Retention:** Insurers initially expected more people to drop their policies before making claims. As more policyholders retain their coverage, costs rise.

Recent data suggests that modern policies experience premium increases of 20-25% every 8-10 years, far more manageable than the 50-100% increases faced by early policyholders.

## Underwriting Requirements

LTCI underwriting is often more stringent than life insurance, as insurers aim to reduce their risk exposure. The application process typically includes:

1. **Health Questionnaire:** A detailed form covering medical history and current conditions.
2. **Phone Interview:** Conducted by a nurse to verify health details and assess cognitive function.
3. **Medical Record Review:** Insurers often request access to your medical records.
4. **Physical Exam:** Occasionally required, depending on age or medical history.
5. **Cognitive Screening:** Older applicants may undergo tests to assess memory and reasoning abilities.

Certain health conditions can disqualify applicants, including:

- Diabetes with complications
- Recent strokes or heart problems
- Mobility limitations requiring walkers or wheelchairs
- Early signs of cognitive impairment
- Progressive diseases like Parkinson's

This is why it's critical to apply while you're still healthy, ideally in your 50s or early 60s.

## Claims Process

Filing a claim begins when you're unable to perform at least two activities of daily living (ADLs) or have a cognitive impairment requiring supervision. The steps include:

1. **Doctor's Certification:** A physician must certify your condition and care needs.
2. **Insurance Assessment:** Insurers typically send a nurse to evaluate your care requirements.
3. **Care Coordination:** Many policies include care coordination services to help you identify and arrange appropriate care.
4. **Benefit Payments:** Once approved, benefits are paid directly to the provider or reimbursed to you, depending on the policy terms.

Navigating this process can feel daunting, but proper documentation and support from a care coordinator or financial advisor can ease the burden.

## Premium Analysis by Age

Premiums for LTCI policies increase significantly as you age, illustrating the financial advantage of purchasing coverage earlier. Here's a typical example for a policy with a $6,000 monthly benefit, three-year benefit period, 90-day elimination period, and 3% compound inflation protection (2025 rates):

- **Age 55:** $2,400-$3,000 annually
- **Age 60:** $3,000-$3,800 annually

- **Age 65:** $4,200-$5,200 annually
- **Age 70:** $6,000-$7,500 annually

These figures demonstrate how waiting just five years can increase your premiums by 20-30%. Additionally, applying earlier reduces the risk of disqualification due to health issues.

## Choosing the Right Policy

Selecting the right LTCI policy requires careful consideration of your financial situation, health status, and preferences. Questions to ask include:

- What are the average care costs in my area?
- Do I want to age in place, or am I open to facility care?
- How much can I afford in premiums?
- Do I need shared care benefits if I'm purchasing coverage with a spouse?

**Susan's Decision**

Remember Susan, who was overwhelmed by LTCI options? After weighing her needs and budget, she chose a policy at age 58 with:

- $6,000 monthly benefit
- Three-year benefit period
- 90-day elimination period
- 3% compound inflation protection

Her annual premium was $2,800—affordable for her budget and significantly less than what she would have paid by waiting until age 65.

**Looking Ahead: Alternative Options**

Traditional LTCI is an excellent choice for many, but it's not the only solution. For those who can't qualify for traditional insurance or prefer alternative approaches, **long-term care annuities** and other hybrid options offer valuable alternatives. These solutions will be explored in the next section, providing additional pathways to fund long-term care and secure your financial future.

When Helen, a 67-year-old retired teacher, came to my office, she was frustrated. Recently declined for traditional long-term care insurance due to her diabetes, she believed her options for safeguarding against long-term care costs were limited. Helen's situation is not uncommon. Health issues, age, or other factors often disqualify individuals from traditional policies. That's when I introduced her to **long-term care annuities**—a powerful, flexible solution that transformed her retirement strategy.

Long-term care (LTC) annuities are hybrid financial products that combine the benefits of an annuity with long-term care coverage. They provide a unique blend of security, flexibility, and accessibility that traditional LTC insurance often cannot match. Let's break down what makes these annuities an increasingly popular choice.

## Types of Long-Term Care Annuities

LTC annuities come in several forms, tailored to meet different financial goals and risk tolerances. Here are the most common types:

**Fixed LTC Annuities**

Fixed LTC annuities offer simplicity and reliability. A single premium payment provides both:

- **Guaranteed LTC Benefits:** These can be 2x or 3x your initial premium. For instance, a $100,000 premium might provide $300,000 in LTC benefits.

- **Death Benefit:** If you don't need long-term care, your heirs receive the remaining value of your annuity.

Fixed LTC annuities are ideal for those who value predictability and want a straightforward way to protect against care costs while leaving a legacy.

**Indexed LTC Annuities**

These annuities link growth to the performance of a financial index, such as the S&P 500. While your principal is protected from losses, market gains can increase the annuity's value over time. Indexed LTC annuities are particularly appealing for individuals concerned about inflation eroding their purchasing power.

**Variable LTC Annuities**

For those with a higher risk tolerance, variable LTC annuities offer growth potential tied to investment portfolios. These products allow for greater returns, but they come with more exposure to market fluctuations. They're suitable for individuals with a longer time horizon or those willing to take on additional risk.

**How Long-Term Care Annuities Work**

LTC annuities differ from traditional LTC insurance in one critical way: they are **dual-purpose products**. This means your investment serves two roles:

1. **Long-Term Care Protection:** If you need care, your annuity provides a pool of funds to cover eligible expenses.

2. **Asset Growth or Legacy Benefit:** If you don't need care, your investment grows over time or passes to your heirs as a death benefit.

## Benefit Triggers

One of the standout advantages of LTC annuities is their straightforward benefit triggers. Unlike traditional LTC insurance, which often involves complex qualification processes, LTC annuities activate benefits when you meet one of two criteria:

1. Inability to perform two of six **activities of daily living (ADLs):**
    - Bathing
    - Dressing
    - Eating
    - Transferring (e.g., moving in and out of bed)
    - Toileting
    - Continence
2. **Cognitive Impairment:** Conditions like Alzheimer's or dementia that require supervision.

Helen, for instance, needed care three years after purchasing her LTC annuity. Her doctor certified her inability to perform two ADLs, and her benefits began within weeks. This simplicity eliminated the delays and confusion often associated with traditional insurance claims.

## Payout Structures

LTC annuities offer flexible payout structures to meet diverse care needs. Typically, benefits are calculated using a **multiplication factor** applied to your initial premium. For example:

- A $200,000 premium with a 3x multiplier provides $600,000 in long-term care benefits.

- Monthly payouts are usually set as a percentage of the total benefit pool. For a $600,000 pool, 2% monthly payouts translate to $12,000—a sufficient amount to cover extensive care in most regions.

Unlike traditional LTC insurance, which often restricts how and where you use benefits, LTC annuities allow funds to be applied to a wide range of care options, including:

- In-home care (often including payments to family caregivers)

- Assisted living

- Nursing home care

- Adult day care

- Home modifications

- Care coordination services

This flexibility is especially valuable for individuals who prefer to age in place or want the freedom to choose their care setting.

**Simplified Qualification**

Traditional LTC insurance is notorious for its stringent underwriting, often excluding applicants with pre-existing conditions. In contrast, LTC annuities feature significantly more lenient qualification requirements:

- **No Medical Exams:** Most applicants only need to complete a health questionnaire and a brief phone interview.
- **No Cognitive Testing:** While older applicants may undergo cognitive screening for insurance, LTC annuities often skip this step.
- **Condition Tolerance:** Applicants with controlled diabetes, well-managed heart issues, or a history of cancer (2-3 years post-treatment) are frequently approved.

Helen, who was declined for traditional LTC insurance due to her diabetes, easily qualified for an LTC annuity. This accessibility makes these products a lifeline for many individuals with health concerns.

## Access to Funds

Another key advantage of LTC annuities is the retained access to your money. Unlike traditional insurance, where premiums are spent and gone, your annuity premium remains an asset you can tap into. Options include:

1. **Surrender Options:** Many contracts allow you to withdraw your premium (minus withdrawals) with minimal surrender charges after a set period.
2. **Emergency Withdrawals:** If unforeseen expenses arise, you can access your funds without

jeopardizing your long-term care benefits.

3. **Regular Withdrawals:** Many annuities allow penalty-free annual withdrawals, often up to 10% of your contract value.

4. **Death Benefits:** If you don't use the long-term care benefits, the remaining value is passed to your beneficiaries, ensuring your money isn't wasted.

Maria, another client, purchased a $150,000 LTC annuity at 65. Five years later, she needed $20,000 for an unexpected medical expense. She withdrew the funds without forfeiting her long-term care protection. This feature is unmatched by traditional insurance.

## Rate Lock Guarantees

LTC annuities offer **rate lock guarantees** that ensure stability and predictability:

- **Benefit Lock:** Once your annuity is purchased, the long-term care multiplier (e.g., 3x) is locked in, guaranteeing benefits regardless of market conditions or claims experience.

- **Growth Lock:** Indexed annuities periodically lock in gains, protecting you from market downturns.

These guarantees eliminate concerns about rising premiums, a common issue in traditional LTC insurance. During periods of market volatility, such as the 2020 economic downturn, LTC annuity holders saw their benefits remain stable or grow, while many traditional policyholders faced rate hikes.

### Cost and Funding Considerations

While LTC annuities require a larger upfront investment, they can be funded in several ways:

- **Retirement Savings:** Many individuals use IRA distributions or other retirement assets to purchase their annuity.
- **1035 Exchange:** If you already own an annuity or life insurance policy, a tax-free 1035 exchange can be used to transfer funds into an LTC annuity.
- **Partial Payments:** Some annuities allow staged funding, making them accessible to those who prefer smaller, incremental investments.

## When LTC Annuities Make Sense

LTC annuities are ideal for individuals who:

1. Value asset flexibility and want to avoid "use-it-or-lose-it" insurance premiums.
2. Have moderate to substantial savings available for an upfront investment.
3. Need lenient underwriting due to health conditions or age.
4. Seek to preserve wealth for heirs while protecting against care costs.

**Case Study: Helen's Success**
Helen invested $200,000 into an LTC annuity, securing $600,000 in long-term care benefits. Two years later, she required care due to her diabetes complications. The process to access benefits was seamless, and she retained control over how and where she received care. Her unused funds remained her asset, providing peace of mind and financial security.

**Conclusion**
Long-term care annuities represent a flexible and secure alternative to traditional insurance. With guaranteed benefits, simplified qualification, and retained access to funds, these products empower retirees to manage long-term care costs without sacrificing financial freedom. For those seeking stability, control, and protection, LTC annuities offer an ideal solution. While they require an upfront investment, their versatility and advantages make them an increasingly popular choice for individuals planning their future care needs.
In the next section, we'll explore hybrid long-term care products, which combine life insurance with LTC benefits. While these products offer additional options, they often lack the flexibility and guaranteed advantages of LTC annuities.

**Hybrid Long-Term Care Products: A Comprehensive Solution**

When Mark and Lisa visited my office, they voiced a concern I hear often: "We want long-term care protection, but we hate the idea of paying premiums for something we might never use." Their hesitation is common, and it reflects a growing desire for solutions that combine financial security with flexibility. This demand has propelled the popularity of **hybrid long-term care products**, which merge the benefits of life insurance or annuities with long-term care (LTC) coverage. These products not only address care needs but also provide value even if long-term care is never required.

## Life Insurance with Long-Term Care Riders

One of the most flexible hybrid solutions is life insurance with long-term care riders. These policies start with a foundation of life insurance, typically universal or whole life, and add an LTC rider that allows policyholders to access the death benefit early to pay for qualified care expenses.

For example, consider a policy with a $300,000 death benefit. If you develop a need for long-term care, the policy might allow you to use up to 2% of the death benefit monthly, providing $6,000 for care while reducing the death benefit proportionally. If you never require care, the full $300,000 passes to your beneficiaries. This dual-purpose structure ensures that your premiums provide value no matter what happens, whether through care benefits or a legacy for your heirs.

Life insurance with LTC riders appeals to those who want a straightforward solution with predictable benefits. Additionally, it can provide significant tax advantages, as both the LTC benefits and the death benefit are typically tax-free.

## Asset-Based Long-Term Care Products

Asset-based LTC products take the hybrid concept further by integrating robust long-term care coverage with guaranteed death benefits. Unlike traditional life insurance with riders, these products are explicitly designed to prioritize LTC benefits while maintaining a secondary focus on legacy protection.

These policies often provide a significant multiplier on your premium. For instance, a $100,000 single premium might yield $400,000 in LTC benefits while preserving a $150,000 death benefit if long-term care isn't needed. The guarantee that benefits won't decrease and premiums won't increase makes asset-based LTC products particularly appealing to retirees seeking predictability.

This certainty, combined with the ability to provide substantial LTC benefits, has made asset-based products a cornerstone of modern retirement planning. Whether purchased as a single premium or through a deferred payment plan, these products allow policyholders to secure their financial future with confidence.

### Flexible Payment Structures

Hybrid products offer two primary payment options, each tailored to different financial preferences and circumstances:

### Single Premium Plans

Single premium plans require an upfront payment, providing immediate protection without ongoing financial obligations. While the initial cost is higher, these plans simplify planning and often deliver better long-term value. For example, a $100,000 single premium might provide $400,000 in LTC benefits and a $150,000 death benefit, ensuring comprehensive coverage in a single transaction.

### Deferred Premium Plans

Deferred premium plans spread the cost over several years, typically 5 to 10, making coverage more accessible for those who prefer smaller, manageable payments. A policy with a $100,000 total premium might allow for annual payments of $10,000 over ten years, providing similar benefits to a single premium plan. This option is particularly attractive for families who want LTC protection but wish to preserve liquidity in the short term.

## Return of Premium Features

Hybrid products stand out for their ability to return premiums if the policy is no longer needed. This feature provides unparalleled peace of mind, ensuring that your investment remains accessible.

Policies often include one or more return-of-premium options:

1. **Full Refund:** Many policies allow 100% of premiums to be returned in the early years, often after a specified period such as five years.

2. **Graduated Refunds:** Partial returns may be available depending on the policy's age and usage history.

3. **Benefit-Adjusted Refunds:** Some products deduct the value of any LTC benefits paid when calculating the refund.

For Mark and Lisa, this feature was a deciding factor. They chose a hybrid product offering a full return of premium after year five, giving them the flexibility to "try it and see."

## Death Benefit Features

Death benefits in hybrid products serve multiple purposes, making them an integral part of the policy's appeal. These benefits ensure that even if LTC benefits are used, your heirs receive a portion of your policy's value. For instance:

- **Residual Death Benefit:** Many policies guarantee a minimum death benefit even after substantial LTC claims.

- **Tax-Advantaged Legacy:** Death benefits are typically paid tax-free, creating an efficient way to transfer wealth.

- **Growth Potential:** Certain products allow the death benefit to grow over time, enhancing its value as a legacy tool.

This combination of care protection and legacy preservation ensures that hybrid products deliver value regardless of your circumstances.

## Immediate Benefit Access

Hybrid products are designed for flexibility and ease of use, offering immediate access to benefits when care is needed. Unlike traditional LTC insurance, which often imposes elimination periods, many hybrid policies waive these delays, enabling you to receive care quickly.
Other features include:

- **Simplified Benefit Triggers:** Benefits typically begin when you're unable to perform two activities of daily living (ADLs) or experience cognitive impairment.

- **Flexible Use:** Funds can be applied to various care settings, including home care, assisted living, and nursing facilities.

- **Quick Claims Processing:** Simplified documentation ensures faster payouts, reducing stress during critical moments.

## Legacy Protection and Liquidity

Hybrid products excel at preserving both your financial flexibility and your legacy. Many policies include features such as:

- **Guaranteed Death Benefits:** Ensuring a portion of your investment is preserved for heirs.

- **Optional Growth Riders:** Enhancing benefits through dividends or market-linked performance.

- **Joint Policies:** Allowing couples to share a single policy, maximizing efficiency and value.

- **Liquidity Options:** These include penalty-free

withdrawals, policy loans, and systematic withdrawals, ensuring that your money remains accessible even in unexpected circumstances.

## Inflation Protection

To address rising care costs, many hybrid products offer inflation protection. Options include:

- **Guaranteed Benefit Increases:** Providing annual growth of 3-5%, compounded to maintain purchasing power.

- **Inflation-Adjusted Payouts:** Benefits adjust at the time of claim to match current care costs.

- **Market-Linked Growth:** Indexed products tie benefit increases to market performance, ensuring robust protection against inflation.

## Tax Advantages

Hybrid products offer significant tax benefits, further enhancing their appeal:

- **Tax-Free Benefits:** Both LTC payouts and death benefits are typically excluded from taxable income.

- **Tax-Deferred Growth:** Cash values grow tax-free until withdrawn.

- **Premium Deductions:** Portions of premiums may qualify for tax deductions in certain situations.

- **1035 Exchanges:** Existing life insurance or annuities can often be converted into hybrid LTC products without tax penalties.

**Simplified Underwriting**

Compared to traditional LTC insurance, hybrid products have lenient underwriting requirements, making them accessible to a broader audience. Applicants with controlled health conditions, such as diabetes or mild heart issues, often qualify with minimal hurdles. Additionally, these policies typically require less medical documentation, offering a streamlined application process.

For example, Richard, who was declined for traditional LTC insurance due to his diabetes, easily qualified for a hybrid policy. With a $150,000 single premium, he secured $450,000 in LTC benefits and a guaranteed death benefit.

**Conclusion**

Hybrid long-term care products are redefining how families plan for aging and unexpected care needs. By combining LTC protection with life insurance or annuity features, they offer unmatched flexibility, guaranteed benefits, and peace of mind. Whether you're focused on preserving wealth, ensuring access to care, or leaving a legacy, hybrid products provide a comprehensive solution tailored to your needs.

Mark and Lisa ultimately chose a 10-pay hybrid policy, spreading their premiums over time while securing immediate protection and premium return options. For them—and many others—this combination of flexibility and security made hybrid products the clear choice. As you consider your own long-term care plan, hybrid products offer a pathway to protection, financial stability, and confidence in the future.

## Deferred Care Benefits and Product Comparisons

When Tom and Martha sat in my office to discuss long-term care options, their initial reaction was one of overwhelm. "How do we know which approach is right for us?" Martha asked. This is a common sentiment, as the array of available options can be daunting. The right choice often hinges on understanding how different products handle **deferred care benefits** and evaluating their features against personal priorities.

## Deferred Care Benefits: Securing Future Protection

Deferred care benefits are a critical feature in many long-term care solutions. They allow individuals to lock in future protection while optimizing costs and flexibility. Let's examine the key aspects of these benefits.

### Future Benefit Growth

One of the most compelling features of deferred care products is the ability to grow benefits over time. For example, traditional long-term care insurance often includes inflation protection riders, with benefits growing at a guaranteed 3-5% annually. This ensures that a policy purchased at age 55 with a $6,000 monthly benefit could provide $12,000 or more by age 75, keeping pace with rising care costs.

Annuities and hybrid products offer alternative growth mechanisms. Indexed products, for instance, can provide average annual growth of 6-8%, linked to market performance, while protecting the principal from losses. These flexible growth opportunities make deferred care products a reliable way to secure future financial stability.

## Premium Payment Options

Deferred care products offer flexibility in how premiums are paid, accommodating a variety of financial circumstances:

1. **Single Premium:** A one-time, larger payment that eliminates future financial obligations. While upfront costs are higher, this approach simplifies planning and often yields better guaranteed benefits.

2. **Limited Pay:** Payments spread over a defined period, typically 5-10 years. This balances affordability with robust coverage, as Tom and Martha discovered when they opted for a 10-year payment plan for a $200,000 premium.

3. **Lifetime Pay:** Smaller, ongoing payments throughout the policyholder's life. While the total cost may be higher, this approach minimizes the immediate financial burden.

4. **Flexible Premium:** Some products allow adjustments to payment amounts and timing, offering further customization.

## Benefit Waiting Periods

Deferred care benefits typically include an elimination period, the waiting time before benefits begin. The choice of elimination period affects both premiums and immediate accessibility to benefits:

- **0 Days:** Benefits start immediately, but premiums are higher.
- **30 Days:** A common balance between cost and quick access to benefits.
- **90 Days:** Often the most cost-effective option, requiring the policyholder to self-fund care for the initial period.
- **180 Days:** Lowest premiums, but necessitates significant self-insurance for the first six months.

Selecting the right waiting period requires an evaluation of available savings and the potential impact of out-of-pocket expenses.

### Inflation Protection

Inflation protection is a cornerstone of deferred care products, ensuring that benefits remain adequate over time. Options include:

- **Compound Interest Riders:** Annual increases of 3-5% that significantly enhance benefit amounts over decades.
- **CPI-Linked Adjustments:** Benefits tied to the Consumer Price Index for real-time cost tracking.
- **Future Purchase Options:** Allowing policyholders to increase benefits at designated

intervals.

- **Market-Based Growth:** Indexed products grow with the market while protecting against losses, appealing to those seeking growth without risk.

## Surrender Provisions and Access Features

Flexibility is a hallmark of modern deferred care products, with many offering access features that balance protection and liquidity:

- **Return of Premium Options:** A guarantee that policyholders can recover unused premiums, often after a set number of years.
- **Partial Withdrawals:** The ability to access a portion of the contract's value when needed.
- **Emergency Access Provisions:** Penalty-free withdrawals in cases of medical or financial emergencies.
- **Systematic Withdrawal Options:** Regular, scheduled withdrawals that don't compromise long-term care benefits.

These features provide policyholders with peace of mind, knowing they retain financial flexibility even as they prepare for future care needs.

## Tax Advantages and Implications

The tax treatment of deferred care products can significantly influence their appeal. Understanding the differences between tax-qualified and non-qualified products is key.

## Tax-Qualified Policies

Tax-qualified products offer several advantages, including:

- **Premium Deductibility:** Premiums may be deductible as medical expenses, subject to IRS limits.
- **Tax-Free Benefits:** All long-term care payouts are excluded from taxable income.
- **Standardized Benefit Triggers:** Clear definitions of eligibility make these policies user-friendly.

### Non-Qualified Policies

Non-qualified policies, while less common, provide:

- **Flexible Benefit Triggers:** Often more lenient than tax-qualified options.
- **Simpler Claims Processes:** Reduced documentation requirements.
- **Broader Coverage:** Policies may include services not covered by tax-qualified options.

## 1035 Exchanges

A **1035 exchange** allows policyholders to transfer funds from an existing life insurance policy or annuity into a new long-term care product without triggering taxes. This is an excellent strategy for those seeking to repurpose underperforming assets for long-term care needs.

## Insurance vs. Annuity Comparison

Understanding the distinctions between traditional long-term care insurance and annuities is essential for informed decision-making. Each product type has its own strengths and limitations.

**Cost Analysis**

- **Traditional Insurance:**
  - Lower initial premiums but ongoing payments.
  - Risk of premium increases over time.
  - Typically no cash value or refunds.
- **Annuities:**
  - Larger upfront investment with no ongoing premiums.
  - Guaranteed premium stability.
  - Maintains cash value that grows over time.

**Benefit Flexibility**

- **Traditional Insurance:**
  - Comprehensive coverage with standardized benefits.
  - Often tied to specific care settings and expenses.
- **Annuities:**
  - Greater flexibility in how benefits are

used.

- o Can cover a broader range of care needs, including home modifications and family caregiving.

**Access to Funds**

- **Traditional Insurance:**
    - o Limited or no access to premiums once paid.
    - o "Use it or lose it" structure, with no residual value.
- **Annuities:**
    - o Policyholders retain access to their principal.
    - o Built-in liquidity and growth potential.
    - o Death benefits provide value even if care isn't needed.

**When Insurance Makes Sense**

Traditional long-term care insurance is ideal for individuals who:

- Are in good health and can qualify for stringent underwriting.
- Want maximum benefits for a lower initial cost.
- Are under 65 and can lock in lower premiums.
- Have a family history of chronic conditions or cognitive decline.

**When Annuities Make Sense**

Annuities are better suited for those who:

- Have significant liquid assets available for a larger initial investment.
- Are over 65 or have minor health issues that might disqualify them from traditional insurance.
- Value liquidity and want access to their funds.
- Seek legacy protection through death benefits.

For example, Lisa, age 62, was concerned about qualifying for traditional insurance due to minor health issues. She invested $150,000 in an LTC annuity, securing $450,000 in care benefits while maintaining access to her funds and leaving a death benefit for her heirs.

**Making the Right Choice**

Choosing the best long-term care product often involves weighing priorities and personal circumstances. Tom and Martha ultimately opted for a hybrid policy because it offered guaranteed premiums, death benefit protection, and return of premium options. This choice balanced their need for financial security, flexibility, and legacy goals.

There is no one-size-fits-all solution to long-term care planning. The optimal approach often combines elements from different products, tailored to meet your unique needs. Whether it's traditional insurance, annuities, or hybrid options, the key is to create a comprehensive plan that secures your future while preserving your financial independence.

## Chapter 4: Self-Funding Strategies

Self-funding long-term care isn't just about having enough money set aside. It's about having the right assets, in the right places, available at the right time. As a financial advisor specializing in retirement planning, I've helped hundreds of families navigate this complex landscape, and I've learned that successful self-funding requires a deep understanding of both strategy and implementation. Let me share what I've learned through years of helping clients create sustainable long-term care funding plans.

The challenge of self-funding has grown more complex in recent years. With increasing longevity, rising care costs, and the evolving healthcare landscape, the strategies that worked a decade ago need significant updating for today's realities. Yet, self-funding remains one of the most flexible approaches to long-term care planning, offering control and adaptability that other funding methods can't match.

## Asset-Based Care Planning

The foundation of successful self-funding starts with understanding exactly what resources you have available and how best to position them for future care needs. Peter, a recent retiree I worked with, thought he had a clear picture of his assets until we sat down together. "I know what I have," he said confidently, showing me his latest 401(k) statement. But as we dug deeper, we discovered resources he hadn't considered and opportunities he'd missed. His story illustrates why comprehensive asset assessment forms the cornerstone of effective self-funding strategies.

## Core Asset Assessment

Let's start with retirement accounts, often representing the largest pool of assets available for long-term care funding. In 2025, the average retiree I work with has between $500,000 and $1.5 million in their combined retirement accounts. These accounts, including traditional IRAs and 401(k)s, offer tax-deferred growth but come with specific rules and restrictions that can impact their use for long-term care.

The tax implications of using retirement accounts for care funding require careful consideration. Consider Sarah's situation. At 68, she had $800,000 in her 401(k) and thought this would be sufficient for any care needs. However, she hadn't considered the tax implications of large withdrawals. When we analyzed her situation, we realized that withdrawing $8,000 monthly for care would require taking out nearly $10,000 to cover the taxes. This discovery led us to develop a more tax-efficient withdrawal strategy combining multiple account types.

Beyond traditional retirement accounts, Roth IRAs deserve special attention in care funding planning. Their tax-free withdrawal features make them particularly valuable for managing income levels when qualifying for various benefits or managing tax brackets during high-expense years. I worked with a couple who strategically converted portions of their traditional IRA to Roth accounts during lower-income years, creating a tax-free pool of funds for future care needs.

## Investment Accounts

Investment accounts offer more flexibility than retirement accounts but require careful management. These taxable accounts – including individual and joint brokerage accounts, mutual fund holdings, and stock portfolios – can provide important tactical advantages in funding care needs. The key lies in structuring these accounts to balance growth potential with accessibility while maintaining tax efficiency.

Consider the case of William and Janet, who had accumulated a significant portfolio of dividend-paying stocks over their careers. We restructured their holdings to create a dedicated care funding portfolio, focusing on high-quality, dividend-growing companies that could provide both income and growth potential. This approach gave them confidence in their ability to fund future care needs while maintaining growth potential for their overall portfolio.

## Savings Accounts and CD's

Savings accounts and CDs play a crucial role in care funding strategies, though their role is more nuanced than many realize. While they offer immediate liquidity, keeping too much in low-yielding accounts can mean missing growth opportunities. The key is finding the right balance between accessibility and growth potential. In today's environment, this often means utilizing a tiered approach to cash management, combining high-yield savings accounts, money market funds, and short-term bond funds to maximize returns while maintaining necessary liquidity.

## Real Estate Holdings

Real estate holdings can serve as powerful tools in long-term care funding, but they require careful planning and management. Primary residences, rental properties, and vacation homes all offer potential funding sources, but each comes with its own complications and considerations. Consider John and Mary, who owned their home outright plus two rental properties. They created a strategy to use rental income for care needs while maintaining the option to sell the property if necessary. Their plan included detailed analysis of property management costs, tax implications, and market conditions to ensure their real estate holdings could reliably support their care funding strategy.

The role of home equity in care funding deserves special attention. While many view their home as a potential source of care funding, accessing this equity requires careful planning. Home equity lines of credit, reverse mortgages, and outright sales each offer different advantages and challenges. I worked with a client who established a home equity line of credit while still working, ensuring access to funds if needed while avoiding the higher costs and complexities of setting up such financing during a crisis.

## Business Interests

Business interests present both unique opportunities and challenges in care funding. Whether it's an ongoing business or one you're planning to sell, understanding how to leverage these assets effectively is crucial. I worked with a small business owner who structured his exit plan specifically to create a care funding pool, using a combination of ongoing consulting payments and installment sale proceeds. This approach provided both reliable income and tax advantages while maintaining some connection to the business he'd built.

## Asset Optimization Strategies

Asset optimization is a comprehensive approach to managing wealth that encompasses several interconnected strategies designed to maximize returns while minimizing tax implications and protecting assets for the long term.

Tax-efficient withdrawal planning is fundamental to preserving wealth during retirement. This strategy involves carefully sequencing withdrawals from different account types to minimize the overall tax burden. Generally, it's advantageous to first draw from taxable accounts, allowing tax-advantaged accounts like traditional IRAs and 401(k)s to continue growing tax-deferred. Additionally, strategic harvesting of capital gains and losses can help offset tax liabilities. For instance, during market downturns, investors can harvest losses to offset gains while maintaining their desired asset allocation through similar but not identical investments.

Asset location strategies focus on placing investments in the most tax-advantaged accounts based on their tax characteristics. High-yield bonds and REITs, which generate regular taxable income, are often better suited for tax-deferred accounts like traditional IRAs. In contrast, growth stocks and municipal bonds typically work well in taxable accounts since they benefit from preferential tax treatment on long-term capital gains and tax-exempt income respectively. This approach can significantly improve after-tax returns without changing the overall investment strategy.

Required Minimum Distribution (RMD) planning becomes crucial for investors aged 73 and older with tax-deferred retirement accounts. Effective RMD strategies often involve starting withdrawals before they become mandatory to smooth out tax implications over time. One advanced technique is using Qualified Charitable Distributions (QCDs), which allow direct transfers from IRAs to qualified charities, satisfying RMD requirements while excluding the amount from taxable income. This can be particularly valuable for philanthropically inclined individuals who want to minimize their adjusted gross income.

Asset protection tools serve as a crucial defense against potential creditors and legal claims. These include insurance products like umbrella policies and specialized trusts. Limited Liability Companies (LLCs) can protect personal assets from business liabilities, while irrevocable trusts can shield assets from future creditors while potentially providing estate tax benefits. For professionals in high-risk fields, combining multiple layers of protection through entities, trusts, and insurance creates a robust defense against potential claims.

Successful asset optimization requires regular review and adjustment of these strategies as circumstances change. Tax laws evolve, personal situations shift, and market conditions fluctuate, necessitating periodic reassessment. For instance, recent changes to retirement account inheritance rules under the SECURE Act have made it more important to consider alternative wealth transfer strategies.

Integration of these strategies is key. For example, when implementing a tax-efficient withdrawal strategy, one must consider how it affects RMD planning and whether it aligns with existing asset protection structures. Similarly, asset location decisions should account for anticipated withdrawal needs and tax implications. A well-coordinated approach ensures these strategies work together seamlessly rather than at cross-purposes.
The complexity of these strategies often necessitates collaboration among financial advisors, tax professionals, and estate planning attorneys to ensure optimal implementation and ongoing management.

Regular coordination among these professionals helps ensure that all aspects of asset optimization work together effectively to achieve the desired outcomes.

## Asset Conversion Options

Asset conversion is the strategic process of transforming one type of asset into another, requiring careful consideration of multiple factors to maximize value while minimizing costs and tax implications. Understanding the complexities of this process is crucial for both individuals and institutions managing wealth.

The concept of liquidation hierarchies forms the foundation of effective asset conversion strategies. Assets should typically be converted in an order that minimizes tax impact and preserves overall portfolio balance. Generally, highly liquid assets with minimal tax consequences should be tapped first, followed by assets with moderate tax implications, leaving assets with the highest tax impact or greatest growth potential until last. This approach helps preserve long-term wealth while meeting immediate liquidity needs.

Tax impact analysis plays a central role in conversion decisions. Converting assets can trigger various tax events, including capital gains, ordinary income, and potential penalties for early withdrawal from retirement accounts. For instance, converting traditional IRA assets to Roth IRAs may result in immediate tax liability but could provide long-term tax advantages. Understanding these implications allows for better timing and structuring of conversions.

Timing considerations extend beyond tax implications. Market conditions, interest rates, and personal circumstances all influence optimal conversion timing. For example, converting assets during market downturns might minimize tax impact while maximizing long-term growth potential in new investment vehicles. Additionally, consideration must be given to seasonal market patterns and economic cycles that might affect asset values.

Conversion costs can significantly impact the overall benefit of asset transformation. These expenses include transaction fees, bid-ask spreads, administrative costs, and professional fees for tax or legal advice. Less obvious costs might include opportunity costs from being out of the market during conversion or potential loss of preferential tax treatment. Understanding and quantifying these costs is essential for determining whether conversion benefits outweigh the associated expenses.

The success of asset conversion strategies often depends on careful coordination of these various elements, requiring regular review and adjustment as circumstances and market conditions change.

## Emergency Fund Considerations for Long-Term Care

An emergency fund tailored to long-term care is an essential part of any comprehensive financial strategy. Unlike a standard emergency fund meant to cover general living expenses during unexpected situations, a long-term care emergency fund addresses specific needs associated with healthcare, caregiving, and related costs. This fund requires a layered approach to ensure sufficient liquidity, growth, and adaptability. In this section, we explore the critical elements of emergency fund planning for long-term care, including liquid reserve requirements, buffer calculations, legacy planning, asset protection, and distribution strategies.

## Liquid Reserve Requirements

Establishing liquid reserve requirements involves understanding the financial needs associated with long-term care and aligning those needs with accessible assets. Liquid reserves ensure funds are available at a moment's notice to cover immediate and ongoing care expenses.

## Short-Term Needs

Short-term needs typically arise during the initial stages of care or emergencies, such as an unexpected hospitalization or the sudden onset of a chronic condition. These funds must be readily accessible to cover expenses like:

- Immediate caregiver hiring.
- Hospital or medical copayments.
- Temporary home modifications, such as grab bars

or ramps.

The ideal short-term reserve is held in highly liquid, low-risk accounts like high-yield savings accounts, money market accounts, or cash equivalents. A typical recommendation is to maintain three to six months' worth of care costs in these accounts. For example, if monthly caregiving expenses are $6,000, a short-term reserve of $18,000 to $36,000 is advisable.

## Intermediate Access

Intermediate access funds address needs that may arise within 6–24 months. These reserves are often used to cover ongoing caregiving expenses, rehabilitation services, or anticipated costs like transitioning from in-home care to an assisted living facility. Funds in this category should provide moderate growth while remaining accessible.
Options for intermediate reserves include:

- Laddered certificates of deposit (CDs): Staggered maturity dates provide regular access to funds.
- Short-term bond funds: These offer higher returns than savings accounts without excessive risk.
- Treasury bills: Highly secure investments with predictable returns.

This layer provides a balance between liquidity and better returns compared to purely short-term reserves. For example, a $60,000 reserve could be divided into six $10,000 CDs maturing every four months, ensuring periodic access to cash while earning interest.

## Long-Term Protection

Long-term protection reserves are designed to fund care needs that might arise years down the road. These reserves should focus on growth potential to outpace inflation while still maintaining some liquidity. Options include:

- Balanced mutual funds: A mix of equities and bonds to balance growth and risk.
- Dividend-paying stocks: Provide a steady income stream while preserving capital.
- Real estate investment trusts (REITs): Offer higher yields and potential capital appreciation.

For individuals in their 50s or early 60s planning for long-term care needs in their 70s or 80s, investing a portion of their reserves in growth-oriented assets can ensure sufficient funding for future costs.

### Buffer Calculations

Buffer calculations ensure that reserves are adequate to cover unexpected cost increases, such as rising care expenses or prolonged care needs. A buffer acts as a financial cushion, accounting for uncertainties and variables that can disrupt even the best-laid plans.
Key factors to consider in buffer calculations include:

- **Inflation:** Healthcare costs historically rise faster than general inflation, often at 3–5% annually. Buffer calculations should factor in these increases over time.
- **Market Volatility:** Investments in stocks or bonds can fluctuate in value, impacting the availability of funds during market downturns.

- **Emergency Scenarios:** Unexpected expenses, such as additional medical treatments or home modifications, should be accounted for.

For example, if annual care costs are projected at $60,000, a 20% buffer would add $12,000, bringing the total reserve requirement to $72,000 annually. This ensures adequate coverage for unforeseen expenses.

## Legacy Planning

Balancing long-term care needs with legacy goals can be challenging but is essential for individuals who wish to leave an inheritance. A well-structured emergency fund should integrate legacy planning strategies to ensure that care costs do not entirely deplete the estate.

## Life Insurance Integration

Permanent life insurance policies can serve as a dual-purpose tool, providing both a death benefit for heirs and liquidity for long-term care. Accelerated death benefits or long-term care riders allow policyholders to access funds while preserving a portion of the benefit for their beneficiaries.

## Trusts for Legacy Protection

Irrevocable trusts can shield assets from being depleted by long-term care costs, ensuring they remain available for heirs. For example, placing real estate or investment accounts into a trust allows them to bypass probate and be protected from creditors.

## Asset Protection

Protecting assets from being entirely consumed by long-term care expenses is a critical aspect of emergency fund planning. Various tools and strategies can safeguard wealth while ensuring sufficient funds are available for care.

**Trust Structures**

- **Irrevocable Trusts:** Protect assets from being considered during Medicaid eligibility assessments.
- **Qualified Personal Residence Trusts (QPRTs):** Preserve the family home while reducing taxable estate value.

**Annuities**

Certain annuities, such as long-term care annuities, offer guaranteed income streams that can cover care costs while protecting the principal.

## Medicaid Planning

For individuals nearing Medicaid eligibility thresholds, strategic asset transfers or the use of Medicaid-compliant annuities can help preserve wealth while qualifying for benefits.

## Distribution Planning

Distribution planning focuses on the sequence and timing of fund withdrawals to maximize longevity and minimize taxes. A well-structured plan prioritizes tax-efficient strategies and aligns with care needs.

## Withdrawal Sequencing

Effective sequencing minimizes tax burdens and optimizes liquidity. For example:

1. Use taxable accounts first to reduce capital gains exposure.
2. Tap tax-deferred accounts, such as traditional IRAs, for predictable income needs.
3. Reserve tax-free accounts, such as Roth IRAs, for high-cost, long-term needs.

## Tax Planning

Long-term care costs are often tax-deductible as medical expenses if they exceed a certain percentage of adjusted gross income (AGI). Incorporating these deductions into withdrawal strategies can reduce overall tax liabilities.

## Review Protocols

Emergency fund plans must be regularly reviewed and adjusted to remain effective. Changing circumstances, such as new healthcare needs or market conditions, can necessitate updates to the plan.

## Annual Reviews

Conducting annual reviews ensures that:

- Reserves are sufficient to meet projected costs.
- Inflation adjustments are factored into calculations.
- Investments align with care needs and risk

tolerance.

**Quarterly Check-Ins**

Regular check-ins allow for timely adjustments to address:

- Market performance and asset allocation.
- Changes in personal circumstances or health status.

**Life Event Triggers**

Major life events, such as a diagnosis of chronic illness or the sale of a property, should prompt an immediate review of the plan to ensure its continued effectiveness.

**Conclusion**

Emergency fund considerations for long-term care require more than a basic savings plan. By implementing a layered approach to liquidity, incorporating buffer calculations, and aligning strategies with legacy goals, individuals can create a robust framework to meet both expected and unexpected care needs. Regular reviews and adjustments ensure the plan remains adaptable, providing peace of mind and financial stability throughout life's uncertainties.

## Chapter 5: Medicaid Planning Essentials

Medicaid is one of the most important programs for individuals needing long-term care, yet it remains one of the most misunderstood. Unlike Medicare, which covers limited long-term care services, Medicaid can provide extensive coverage for nursing home care, home health services, and other long-term care needs. However, accessing Medicaid benefits requires navigating complex eligibility requirements, particularly income limits. This section explains these requirements in detail, offering practical insights and strategies to help individuals and families plan effectively.

## Eligibility Requirements Explained

Medicaid eligibility varies by state, but the general framework remains consistent nationwide. Applicants must meet specific financial thresholds, including income and asset limits. While asset requirements focus on the value and type of assets owned, income limits play an equally significant role in determining eligibility for long-term care benefits.

## Income Limits

Medicaid's income limits are designed to ensure that benefits are reserved for those with the greatest financial need. These limits are strict, and exceeding them—even by a small amount—can result in denial of benefits. Understanding the nuances of these income rules is essential for effective Medicaid planning.

## Monthly Income Thresholds

Each state sets monthly income thresholds for Medicaid eligibility, which typically align with the federal poverty level (FPL). For institutional care, such as nursing home coverage, the monthly income limit in 2025 is often around $2,742 for a single individual. However, thresholds can vary by state and by the type of care requested. For example, some states have higher income limits for individuals applying for home- and community-based services compared to institutional care.

For married couples, Medicaid applies different rules depending on whether one or both spouses are seeking coverage. For example, if only one spouse requires Medicaid, the other, referred to as the "community spouse," may retain a larger portion of the couple's income to ensure they can maintain a reasonable standard of living.

## Countable vs. Non-Countable Income

Medicaid evaluates all sources of income to determine eligibility, dividing them into two categories: countable and non-countable income.

1. **Countable Income**

   This includes all regular income sources such as:

- Social Security benefits
- Pension payments
- Wages or self-employment income
- Interest, dividends, and other investment income
- Annuity payouts

Countable income is the primary measure used to determine whether an applicant exceeds Medicaid's income thresholds.

2. **Non-Countable Income**
   Certain types of income are excluded from Medicaid's calculations. These often include:
   - Some veterans' benefits
   - Income used for specific medical expenses
   - Supplemental Security Income (SSI), in some cases
   - Irregular or one-time payments, depending on state rules

Understanding which types of income are countable versus non-countable allows applicants to adjust their finances strategically to meet eligibility requirements.

**Miller Trust/Qualified Income Trust**
For individuals whose income exceeds Medicaid's monthly thresholds, states often allow the use of a Miller Trust, also known as a Qualified Income Trust (QIT). These trusts are designed to help applicants redirect excess income, ensuring they meet Medicaid's income requirements.

## How a Miller Trust Works

1. The individual establishes the trust with assistance from an attorney or financial professional.
2. Income exceeding Medicaid's threshold is deposited into the trust each month.
3. Funds in the trust are used to pay for allowable expenses, such as nursing home care or other medical costs.

By removing the excess income from the individual's direct control, a Miller Trust effectively reduces their countable income, enabling them to qualify for Medicaid benefits.

**Practical Example:**
John receives $3,000 monthly from Social Security and a pension, exceeding his state's Medicaid income limit of $2,742. To qualify, he deposits $258 into a Miller Trust each month. The funds are then used to pay for his nursing home care, satisfying Medicaid's requirements while preserving his eligibility.

## Treatment of Social Security

Social Security benefits are one of the most common sources of income for retirees and are always considered countable income under Medicaid rules. For many applicants, Social Security payments alone can push them over the income threshold, making proper planning critical.

Strategies to address Social Security income include:

- Allocating excess funds to a Miller Trust, as discussed above.

- Structuring income distributions to maximize allowable deductions, such as medical expenses not covered by Medicaid.

- For married couples, shifting some of the income to the community spouse under spousal impoverishment rules, which allow the non-applicant spouse to retain a portion of the applicant's income for their living expenses.

## Pension and Retirement Income Rules

Pension payments and retirement distributions are also counted as income for Medicaid eligibility. This includes:

- Defined benefit pensions, which provide monthly payments based on years of service and salary.

- Required Minimum Distributions (RMDs) from retirement accounts like IRAs or 401(k)s.

For individuals with significant pension or retirement income, exceeding Medicaid's income limits is common. Strategies to address this include:

- Redirecting income to a Miller Trust.

- Electing spousal income allowances to shift a portion of the income to the community spouse.
- Managing RMD schedules to minimize taxable income while meeting required withdrawal amounts.

**Example:**
Linda, a retired teacher, receives a $4,000 monthly pension, exceeding her state's Medicaid income limit. By establishing a Miller Trust and depositing $1,500 monthly into the account, she becomes eligible for Medicaid without forfeiting her pension.

**Interest and Investment Income**

Interest and dividends from investments, such as stocks, bonds, or mutual funds, are considered countable income. This includes:

- Interest from savings accounts or CDs.
- Dividends from equity investments.
- Capital gains distributed by mutual funds.

Planning for investment income involves strategies to reduce taxable events and manage distributions effectively:

- Transitioning to tax-efficient investments, such as municipal bonds or tax-managed mutual funds.
- Using Roth IRAs for tax-free distributions.
- Allocating investment income toward deductible medical expenses to reduce countable income.

**Practical Example:**
Sam holds $300,000 in dividend-paying stocks, generating $10,000 annually in income. By reallocating part of his portfolio to municipal bonds, he reduces his countable income by $5,000 annually, bringing him closer to Medicaid's income eligibility threshold.

**Key Takeaways**
Navigating Medicaid's income limits is one of the most challenging aspects of qualifying for benefits, but it is also one of the most critical. By understanding monthly income thresholds, the distinction between countable and non-countable income, and the role of tools like Miller Trusts, individuals can strategically position their finances to access the care they need. Additionally, addressing the treatment of Social Security, pensions, and investment income through careful planning ensures compliance with Medicaid's rules while preserving financial security.

Proper Medicaid planning requires a proactive approach. Working with financial advisors, elder law attorneys, and Medicaid specialists can help individuals and families create a tailored strategy that aligns with their unique circumstances, ensuring access to essential long-term care benefits while protecting their assets.

## Asset Limits and Medical Necessity Criteria for Medicaid Planning

Medicaid serves as a critical resource for long-term care, but understanding its requirements can be overwhelming. Two key components—**asset limits** and **medical necessity criteria**—determine eligibility. This chapter explores these aspects in detail, offering insights into how individuals and families can navigate the complexities of Medicaid planning.

## Asset Limits

Medicaid imposes strict asset limits to ensure that benefits are reserved for those with the greatest financial need. These limits vary depending on whether the applicant is single or married, the type of assets involved, and the rules governing specific asset categories.

## Individual Limits

For single individuals applying for Medicaid long-term care services, the asset limit is typically low, often around **$2,000** in countable assets. However, this threshold can vary by state and program. Countable assets include bank accounts, stocks, bonds, and other liquid resources. Assets exceeding the limit must often be "spent down" on care-related expenses before eligibility is granted.

## Spend-Down Strategies

Spend-down strategies allow individuals to reduce their countable assets in ways that comply with Medicaid rules. Examples include:

- Paying off outstanding debts.

- Purchasing exempt assets, such as a primary residence or vehicle.
- Prepaying funeral expenses (discussed later in this chapter).

Proper documentation is essential to ensure these transactions are viewed as legitimate and not as attempts to transfer assets to avoid Medicaid rules.

## Couple Limits

When one spouse requires Medicaid long-term care and the other does not, different asset limits apply. Medicaid aims to prevent the "community spouse" (the spouse not receiving care) from becoming impoverished.

**Community Spouse Resource Allowance (CSRA)**

The **CSRA** allows the community spouse to retain a portion of the couple's combined assets, typically between **$29,724 and $148,620** (2025 figures). The exact amount varies by state. The applicant spouse must still meet the $2,000 asset limit.

**Example:**

John and Mary have $100,000 in combined assets. John applies for Medicaid long-term care. Medicaid rules allow Mary to retain up to $50,000 under the CSRA, while John must spend down his share of the assets to $2,000 before qualifying.

**Community Spouse Rules**

In addition to asset protections, Medicaid provides income protections for the community spouse. These rules allow the community spouse to retain a portion of the couple's monthly income to ensure financial stability.

**Monthly Maintenance Needs Allowance (MMNA)**

The **MMNA** allows the community spouse to retain income between **$2,465 and $3,715** per month (2025 figures), depending on state guidelines. If the community spouse's income falls below this level, they may receive a portion of the applicant spouse's income to meet the allowance.

**Exempt vs. Non-Exempt Assets**

Medicaid distinguishes between **exempt assets** (not counted toward eligibility limits) and **non-exempt assets** (counted toward limits). Understanding this distinction is critical for effective planning.

## Exempt Assets

Exempt assets include:

- **Primary residence**: Typically exempt if the applicant intends to return home or if a spouse, minor child, or disabled adult child lives there. Some states impose an equity limit, often around **$688,000 to $1,033,000**.

- **One vehicle**: Regardless of value, a single vehicle is usually exempt.

- **Personal property**: Household goods and personal effects, such as furniture and clothing, are not counted.

- **Prepaid funeral plans**: Irrevocable funeral trusts or burial plans are exempt.
- **Certain life insurance policies**: Policies with a face value under a specified threshold (e.g., $1,500) are typically exempt.

## Non-Exempt Assets

Non-exempt assets include:

- Bank accounts and cash reserves.
- Stocks, bonds, and mutual funds.
- Additional vehicles beyond the one exempt vehicle.
- Non-primary real estate, such as rental properties or vacation homes.

## Business Asset Treatment

For individuals owning a business, Medicaid rules can be complex. Some states allow certain business assets to be exempt if they are essential to the business's operation.

**Examples of Exempt Business Assets:**

- Equipment, machinery, and tools necessary for the business.
- Inventory required for operations.
- Real estate directly used for the business (e.g., farmland).

Proper documentation and proof of operational necessity are required to ensure these assets are not included in Medicaid's asset calculations.

## Vehicle and Personal Property Rules

As noted, one vehicle is generally exempt, regardless of its value. Additional vehicles may be counted unless they serve specific purposes, such as medical transportation. Household goods and personal property are also exempt but must be reasonably valued to avoid scrutiny.

## Medical Necessity Criteria

In addition to financial requirements, Medicaid applicants must meet medical necessity criteria. These criteria ensure that long-term care benefits are provided to individuals who genuinely need them.

## Level of Care Requirements

To qualify for Medicaid long-term care, applicants must demonstrate that they require a **nursing home level of care (NHLOC)** or equivalent. This often includes:

- Assistance with **activities of daily living (ADLs)** such as bathing, dressing, eating, or toileting.
- Skilled medical care, such as wound care or physical therapy.

Each state establishes specific criteria for determining the level of care, which may involve scoring systems or assessments.

## Assessment Process

Medicaid uses a standardized assessment process to evaluate applicants' care needs. This process often includes:

- **Functional assessments**: Evaluating the individual's ability to perform ADLs.
- **Cognitive assessments**: Identifying conditions like dementia or Alzheimer's.
- **Medical evaluations**: Documenting chronic conditions and treatment requirements.

Assessments are typically conducted by state-approved agencies, and results are used to determine eligibility for Medicaid long-term care services.

## Documentation Needs

Comprehensive documentation is essential for meeting Medicaid's medical necessity criteria. Required documents may include:

- Medical records from physicians and specialists.
- Hospital discharge summaries.
- Functional assessment forms completed by care providers.
- Prescription records indicating ongoing treatment needs.

Incomplete or missing documentation can delay the approval process, making meticulous record-keeping critical.

## Physician Certification

A physician's certification is often required to confirm the applicant's medical necessity for long-term care. This certification must:

- State the applicant's specific medical conditions.
- Detail the care required to address these conditions.
- Explain why the applicant cannot receive adequate care at home.

## Reassessment Timelines

Once approved for Medicaid, recipients must undergo periodic reassessments to confirm continued eligibility. These reassessments typically occur annually but may be required more frequently if the recipient's condition improves or changes.

## Appeal Rights

If Medicaid denies an application based on medical necessity criteria, applicants have the right to appeal. The appeals process involves:

- Requesting a fair hearing within the specified timeframe (often 30–90 days).
- Providing additional evidence, such as updated medical records or physician statements.
- Seeking legal or professional representation for complex cases.

## Prepaid Funeral Plans

Prepaid funeral plans offer a strategic way to spend down assets while ensuring end-of-life expenses are covered. Medicaid exempts irrevocable funeral trusts and burial plots, allowing applicants to allocate funds without impacting eligibility.

### Medical Equipment

Medicaid often covers the cost of durable medical equipment (DME), such as wheelchairs, hospital beds, and oxygen tanks. Applicants must demonstrate medical necessity for the equipment, which typically requires:

- A physician's prescription.
- Documentation of the specific medical condition the equipment addresses.

## Personal Property

Personal property, including clothing, jewelry, and household items, is generally exempt from Medicaid's asset calculations. However, high-value items, such as collectibles or antiques, may be scrutinized and counted toward asset limits.

### Debt Reduction

Paying off debts, such as mortgages, credit card balances, or medical bills, is an effective strategy for reducing countable assets. Medicaid allows this as a legitimate spend-down method, provided it is documented appropriately.

**Conclusion**

Navigating Medicaid's asset limits and medical necessity criteria requires a deep understanding of the rules and proactive planning. By leveraging exempt assets, using trusts, and ensuring proper documentation, individuals can qualify for benefits while preserving their financial security. Strategic planning, combined with professional guidance, ensures access to essential long-term care services without unnecessary financial hardship.

## Common Medicaid Planning Mistakes

Planning for Medicaid eligibility is a critical step for individuals and families facing the high costs of long-term care. However, navigating the intricate rules and regulations of Medicaid can lead to significant errors if not handled correctly. Mistakes in timing, documentation, or strategy can delay eligibility, result in penalties, or even disqualify an applicant. This section explores common Medicaid planning mistakes and offers insights on how to avoid them.

## Timing Errors

Timing plays a crucial role in Medicaid planning. Many mistakes stem from either procrastination or poor execution of strategies. Properly timing asset transfers, applications, and assessments is critical to ensure compliance with Medicaid's strict requirements.

## Late Planning Start

One of the most common Medicaid planning mistakes is starting the process too late. Many individuals and families underestimate the time required to qualify for Medicaid, especially when they need long-term care immediately. Starting late often limits the available strategies, leaving families scrambling to spend down assets or manage documentation at the last minute.

For example, someone who delays planning until they are admitted to a nursing home may find that they need to spend down significant resources quickly, losing opportunities to protect assets through trusts or exemptions. Early planning—ideally several years before care is needed—allows for greater flexibility and better outcomes.

## Improper Transfer Timing

Improperly timed asset transfers are another frequent issue. Medicaid imposes a **five-year look-back period** for asset transfers, meaning any gifts or transfers for less than fair market value made within five years of applying for Medicaid are subject to penalties. Many individuals attempt to transfer assets to family members too close to the application date, triggering a penalty period during which Medicaid will not cover care.

Proper planning involves strategic transfers well before the five-year look-back period begins. For instance, transferring assets into an irrevocable trust five or more years before applying can protect them from Medicaid calculations while avoiding penalties.

## Look-Back Violations

The look-back period is one of the most misunderstood aspects of Medicaid planning. Violations occur when individuals attempt to hide or improperly transfer assets during the five years prior to applying for Medicaid. Examples include:

- Gifting large sums of money to family members.
- Selling assets below fair market value.
- Failing to report transfers accurately.

Violations result in penalty periods calculated based on the total amount transferred divided by the average monthly cost of nursing home care in the applicant's state. For example, if $50,000 was improperly transferred and the average monthly cost is $5,000, the penalty period would be 10 months, delaying Medicaid eligibility.

## Application Timing

Timing the Medicaid application incorrectly can also cause problems. Applying too early, before spend-down requirements are met, may result in denial. Conversely, waiting too long to apply can create a gap in coverage, forcing families to pay out-of-pocket for care.

For example, if an individual needs care in March but doesn't apply until June, they may be responsible for several months of care costs. Properly assessing the timing of spend-down strategies and aligning them with the application process ensures seamless coverage.

## Resource Assessment Errors

Medicaid requires a thorough assessment of all assets to determine eligibility. Failing to properly assess resources can lead to delays or denials. Common errors include:

- Misclassifying assets as exempt or non-exempt.
- Forgetting to disclose certain accounts or properties.
- Overlooking jointly held assets or accounts.

A professional assessment of resources helps identify potential issues and ensures accurate reporting to Medicaid, reducing the likelihood of errors.

## Documentation Failures

Medicaid's application process requires comprehensive documentation to verify eligibility. Missing, incomplete, or inconsistent records are among the leading causes of application delays and denials.

## Insufficient Records

Medicaid applications require a complete accounting of income, assets, and expenses. Insufficient records can derail the process, leading to requests for additional information or outright denial. For example, applicants must provide:

- Bank statements for all accounts.
- Proof of income, such as Social Security benefit letters or pension statements.
- Property deeds and mortgage information.

Failing to gather and submit these records promptly can significantly delay the application process.

## Missing Contracts

Caregiver agreements, promissory notes, and other legal contracts are often overlooked in Medicaid applications. These documents are essential for justifying certain transactions, such as payments to family members for caregiving services. Without these agreements, Medicaid may classify such payments as improper transfers, triggering penalties.

For example, a mother paying her daughter $1,000 monthly for caregiving must have a written caregiver agreement specifying the services provided and the payment terms. Otherwise, Medicaid may treat the payments as gifts.

## Incomplete Gift History

Medicaid requires a detailed history of gifts or transfers made within the five-year look-back period. Failing to document these transactions adequately can result in penalties. Applicants must provide:

- Dates and amounts of all gifts or transfers.
- Names of recipients.
- Purpose of the transactions.

Even small gifts, such as holiday or birthday money, should be accounted for to avoid discrepancies during the review process.

## Inadequate Explanations

Certain transactions or financial changes require detailed explanations to satisfy Medicaid's requirements. For example:

- Large bank withdrawals may need documentation showing they were used for legitimate expenses, such as home repairs or medical bills.
- Asset sales must include proof that they were conducted at fair market value.

Without clear explanations and supporting evidence, Medicaid may assume the worst-case scenario, leading to penalties or denial.

## Poor Record Keeping

Poor record keeping often creates issues during the Medicaid application process. Applicants who cannot produce the necessary documentation face delays, additional scrutiny, or even denial. Common examples of poor record keeping include:

- Misplacing old bank statements.
- Failing to keep receipts for large expenses.
- Overlooking documentation for financial transactions made years earlier.

Implementing a systematic approach to record keeping—such as maintaining digital copies of all financial documents—ensures smoother navigation of Medicaid's documentation requirements.

## How to Avoid Documentation Failures

1. **Maintain Comprehensive Records:** Keep organized files of all financial documents, including bank statements, investment records, property deeds, and tax returns.

2. **Work with Professionals:** Engage an elder law attorney or Medicaid planner to review and organize documentation before applying.

3. **Create a Financial Timeline:** Track significant financial events, such as gifts, transfers, and large purchases, to ensure accurate reporting during the application process.

4. **Use Digital Tools:** Scan and store documents electronically for easy access and backup.

## The Importance of Professional Guidance

Avoiding common Medicaid planning mistakes often requires professional assistance. Elder law attorneys and Medicaid specialists can provide valuable guidance on timing strategies, asset transfers, and documentation requirements. They ensure compliance with Medicaid rules while maximizing asset protection, giving families peace of mind during the planning process.

**Conclusion**

Medicaid planning is a complex process that requires meticulous attention to detail and careful timing. Mistakes in timing and documentation are common but avoidable with the right strategies. By starting the planning process early, properly timing asset transfers, and maintaining comprehensive records, individuals and families can navigate Medicaid's requirements successfully. Proactive planning not only ensures eligibility but also preserves assets and reduces financial stress during a challenging time.

## Long-Term Care Strategy Mistakes

Planning for long-term care often involves complex strategies designed to preserve assets, ensure eligibility for Medicaid, and provide financial security during care. However, errors in executing these strategies can lead to delays, penalties, or even disqualification from benefits. This section explores common long-term care strategy mistakes, including choosing the wrong trust type, improper gifting, poor asset conversion, incorrect spend-down practices, and invalid agreements.

## Wrong Trust Type

Trusts are a powerful tool in long-term care planning, but selecting the wrong type can undermine your entire strategy. Irrevocable trusts are commonly used for Medicaid planning because assets placed in these trusts are no longer considered the applicant's property. However, failing to create the appropriate trust or misunderstanding its rules can lead to costly errors.

For example, using a **revocable trust** instead of an irrevocable one can disqualify an applicant from Medicaid. Revocable trusts allow the grantor to retain control over the assets, meaning they are still considered countable for Medicaid eligibility. On the other hand, irrevocable trusts remove assets from the grantor's estate, protecting them from being counted, provided the trust is established outside the five-year look-back period.

Mistakes often arise when trusts are not structured correctly. For instance, an irrevocable trust must clearly outline the restrictions on accessing principal and income to comply with Medicaid requirements. Failure to properly draft or manage the trust can lead to penalties or legal challenges.

## Improper Gifting

Gifting assets to family members is a common approach to reducing countable resources, but improper gifting can trigger Medicaid penalties. Medicaid imposes a **five-year look-back period** on gifts, meaning any assets transferred for less than fair market value within five years of applying for benefits may result in a penalty period.

For example, giving a $50,000 gift to a child three years before applying for Medicaid would be considered an improper transfer. Medicaid calculates penalties by dividing the total amount gifted by the average monthly cost of nursing home care in the applicant's state. This penalty period delays eligibility, forcing families to pay for care out-of-pocket during that time.

To avoid improper gifting, all transfers must be carefully planned and documented. Establishing a gifting strategy early—well before the five-year look-back period—is essential. Additionally, working with an elder law attorney can ensure gifts are structured to comply with Medicaid rules and avoid penalties.

## Poor Asset Conversion

Asset conversion strategies, such as transferring countable assets into exempt categories, are vital for Medicaid planning. However, poor execution can lead to significant problems. Common errors include converting assets too late, failing to consider tax consequences, or misunderstanding the exempt asset rules.

For example, converting cash into a prepaid funeral plan is often a legitimate Medicaid strategy. However, purchasing a revocable funeral plan instead of an irrevocable one would make the asset countable, disqualifying the applicant. Similarly, purchasing a second vehicle without understanding Medicaid's one-vehicle exemption rule would result in the asset being counted.

Another example of poor asset conversion is liquidating a retirement account to pay for care without considering tax implications. The withdrawal could trigger a significant tax liability, reducing the funds available for care and complicating Medicaid eligibility.

## Incorrect Spend-Down

Spend-down strategies are necessary to reduce countable assets to meet Medicaid eligibility limits. However, incorrect spend-down practices can result in disqualification or penalties. Common mistakes include spending assets on non-allowable expenses, failing to document expenditures, or overlooking opportunities to use exempt categories.

For instance, using countable assets to pay off a child's mortgage or make gifts would violate Medicaid's rules, triggering penalties. On the other hand, using the same funds to pay for medical expenses, home modifications, or prepaid funeral arrangements would be allowable and would not affect eligibility.
An effective spend-down strategy requires a detailed plan that aligns with Medicaid's rules. Working with a financial advisor or Medicaid specialist can help families identify allowable expenses and ensure proper documentation of all transactions.

## Invalid Agreements

Informal financial arrangements, such as caregiver contracts or loans to family members, are often overlooked but can lead to problems during Medicaid eligibility reviews. Medicaid requires formal agreements to ensure transactions are legitimate and not disguised gifts.

For example, paying a family member to provide care without a written caregiver agreement can result in those payments being classified as gifts. A valid caregiver agreement must include:

- A detailed description of the services provided.

- The hourly or monthly rate paid.
- A clear timeframe for the arrangement.

Similarly, loans to family members must have formal, written agreements outlining repayment terms, including interest rates and schedules. Without proper documentation, Medicaid may treat the loan as a gift, triggering penalties.

Invalid agreements can also arise when individuals attempt to transfer assets into trusts or partnerships without consulting legal professionals. Improperly drafted or executed agreements can be challenged during Medicaid's review process, resulting in delays or denial of benefits.

## Avoiding Strategy Mistakes

To avoid these common long-term care strategy mistakes, it's essential to:

1. **Start Planning Early**: Begin planning at least five years before care is needed to avoid look-back penalties and ensure sufficient time for strategic asset transfers.

2. **Work with Professionals**: Engage an elder law attorney or Medicaid specialist to ensure strategies comply with state-specific rules and regulations.

3. **Document Everything**: Maintain comprehensive records of all transactions, agreements, and plans to provide clarity during the Medicaid application process.

4. **Review Strategies Regularly**: Regularly revisit your long-term care plan to account for changes in laws, finances, or family circumstances.

By carefully planning and executing strategies, families can navigate the complexities of long-term care funding while preserving assets and avoiding costly mistakes.

# Long-Term Care Planning Timeline and Checklist

Planning for long-term care requires a well-structured approach to ensure that financial, legal, and practical needs are addressed before care is required. Starting early allows for more flexibility in protecting assets and developing strategies that align with Medicaid rules and regulations. This section outlines a comprehensive timeline and checklist for long-term care planning, divided into three critical phases: five years out, two to three years out, and the final year before applying for benefits.

## Five Years Out: Laying the Foundation

The five-year mark is a crucial starting point for long-term care planning, as Medicaid enforces a **five-year look-back period** on all financial transactions. During this phase, the focus is on establishing a clear understanding of financial resources, developing strategies, and initiating asset protection measures.

### Initial Assessment

The planning process begins with a thorough assessment of current financial, medical, and personal circumstances. This includes:

- Evaluating income sources, such as Social Security, pensions, and investment dividends.
- Reviewing asset holdings, including real estate, retirement accounts, and personal property.

- Identifying potential long-term care needs based on family medical history and current health conditions.

For example, a couple with $1 million in assets might need to determine how much they can protect while qualifying for Medicaid. This assessment establishes a baseline for strategy development.

## Strategy Development

After completing the initial assessment, the next step is to develop a comprehensive strategy tailored to the individual's or family's circumstances. Key components of this strategy include:

- Determining whether to use trusts, annuities, or other tools to protect assets.
- Identifying allowable expenses for spend-down purposes, such as home improvements or prepaid funeral plans.
- Establishing goals for legacy planning, such as leaving assets for children or charitable causes.

For example, creating a plan to transfer $200,000 into an irrevocable trust over five years can shield those assets from Medicaid calculations while maintaining flexibility for care needs.

## Transfer Planning

Asset transfers should begin as early as possible to avoid penalties during the look-back period. This includes:

- Transferring ownership of non-exempt assets to an irrevocable trust.

- Gifting allowable amounts to family members or beneficiaries.
- Converting countable assets into exempt categories, such as purchasing a primary residence or paying down mortgage debt.

For instance, transferring $10,000 annually to children within the allowable gift tax limits avoids triggering tax liabilities while reducing countable resources.

## Documentation Start

Proper documentation is critical to a successful Medicaid application. Begin creating a comprehensive file that includes:

- Financial statements from all accounts.
- Property deeds and valuations.
- Records of any asset transfers, including dates, amounts, and recipients.

Maintaining organized records ensures compliance with Medicaid's strict documentation requirements and reduces the likelihood of delays or denials.

## Two to Three Years Out: Refining the Plan

At the two- to three-year mark, the focus shifts to implementing advanced planning strategies and ensuring assets are structured to maximize protection. This phase is critical for fine-tuning the plan and addressing any gaps.

## Asset Restructuring

Restructuring assets to align with Medicaid's eligibility rules is essential. This process may involve:

- Converting liquid assets into exempt categories, such as purchasing a single exempt vehicle.

- Ensuring home equity does not exceed Medicaid's allowable limits (varies by state).

- Dividing jointly held assets between spouses to maximize the community spouse resource allowance.

For example, a single individual might sell a vacation property and use the proceeds to fund allowable expenses, such as home modifications or medical equipment.

## Trust Implementation

If an irrevocable trust has not yet been established, this is the time to create and fund it. Key steps include:

- Working with an elder law attorney to draft the trust.

- Transferring assets into the trust, ensuring compliance with Medicaid's rules.

- Reviewing the trust periodically to ensure it remains aligned with long-term goals.

For instance, a trust might hold $300,000 in investments while allowing the applicant to benefit from the income without jeopardizing Medicaid eligibility.

## Contract Development

Formal contracts are essential for transactions that could be scrutinized by Medicaid, such as:

- Caregiver agreements with family members providing in-home care.
- Promissory notes for loans to family or friends.
- Rental agreements for shared living arrangements.

A properly drafted caregiver agreement, for example, might specify the services provided, the hourly rate, and the total payment amount. This ensures payments are not treated as gifts during Medicaid's review.

## Spend-Down Planning

Spend-down strategies must comply with Medicaid's rules to avoid penalties. Examples of allowable spend-down expenses include:

- Paying off debts, such as credit card balances or mortgages.
- Making necessary home repairs or modifications.
- Purchasing medical equipment, such as wheelchairs or hospital beds.

Coordinating spend-down activities with the broader asset protection strategy ensures resources are used effectively while meeting Medicaid requirements.

## Final Year: Preparing for Application

In the final year before applying for Medicaid, the focus shifts to completing all necessary documentation, ensuring eligibility, and planning for the transition to care services. This phase requires careful attention to detail to avoid errors that could delay or jeopardize benefits.

## Documentation Completion

Ensure that all required documentation is complete and up to date. This includes:

- Finalizing financial records for the past five years.
- Verifying the accuracy of all asset transfers and spend-down activities.
- Gathering proof of medical necessity for long-term care, such as physician certifications and care assessments.

For example, providing five years of bank statements with clear explanations of all transactions demonstrates compliance with Medicaid's look-back rules.

## Application Preparation

Preparing the Medicaid application involves assembling all necessary forms and supporting documents. Key steps include:

- Completing the Medicaid application accurately and thoroughly.
- Including all required supporting materials, such as financial records and medical documentation.
- Working with a Medicaid specialist or attorney to

review the application for accuracy.

Submitting an incomplete or inaccurate application can result in delays or denials, so attention to detail is critical.

## Provider Selection

Selecting a long-term care provider that aligns with Medicaid's requirements is an important step. Considerations include:

- Ensuring the facility is Medicaid-certified.
- Evaluating the quality of care and services provided.
- Reviewing the facility's policies on Medicaid patients.

For instance, researching and visiting local nursing homes or assisted living facilities helps families make informed decisions about care options.

## Transition Planning

Transitioning to care services involves logistical and emotional preparation. Steps include:

- Coordinating the move to a care facility or arranging in-home care.
- Notifying family members and caregivers of the transition timeline.
- Ensuring all medical and personal needs are addressed during the transition.

Having a detailed transition plan reduces stress for both the individual receiving care and their family members.

## Conclusion

A well-executed long-term care planning timeline ensures individuals and families are prepared to meet Medicaid's eligibility requirements while protecting assets and securing quality care. By starting five years out, refining strategies two to three years out, and completing preparations in the final year, families can navigate the complexities of Medicaid planning with confidence. Regular reviews and professional guidance throughout the process ensure plans remain effective and aligned with evolving circumstances.

# Chapter 6: Family Conversations and Decisions

## Starting the Care Conversation

Starting the conversation about long-term care with family members can feel daunting, but it is a critical step in creating a sustainable care plan. These discussions often touch on sensitive topics, such as financial resources, medical needs, and caregiving responsibilities. Taking a thoughtful approach to timing, setting, and goals can ensure the conversation is productive and supportive rather than overwhelming.

## Initial Approach

The success of a long-term care conversation often hinges on how and when it is initiated. A rushed, poorly timed, or emotionally charged discussion can lead to confusion, defensiveness, or family conflict. By carefully planning the timing, choosing the right setting, identifying key participants, and defining clear goals, families can create a foundation for constructive dialogue.

## Timing and Setting

Choosing the right time and place for the care conversation is critical. Timing considerations include assessing when family members are emotionally prepared, as well as ensuring the conversation doesn't coincide with major life events or crises. For instance, discussing long-term care needs immediately after a health scare might seem logical but could lead to heightened emotions that derail the conversation. Instead, aim for a time when everyone involved can approach the discussion with clarity and focus.

The physical setting also plays a significant role. Opt for a neutral, comfortable location that allows for privacy and limits distractions. For example, a quiet living room or a family member's home might provide the relaxed atmosphere needed for a sensitive conversation. Avoid public places like restaurants, where privacy is limited, or virtual meetings, where emotional nuances may be lost.
Timing and setting are also about the length of the discussion. Plan for a manageable time frame, such as an hour or two, to ensure that everyone can stay engaged without feeling overwhelmed. Complex issues that require extended conversations can be broken into multiple sessions, allowing time for reflection and follow-up.

## Key Participants

The success of any family care conversation depends on having the right people involved. Identifying and including key participants early ensures that all voices are heard, and no critical perspectives are overlooked.

1. **Immediate Family Members:** At minimum, involve the person requiring care (if possible) and

their immediate family, such as adult children or spouses. The care recipient's preferences and priorities must remain central to the discussion.

2. **Primary Decision-Makers:** Designate individuals who will take on active roles in decision-making and caregiving. For instance, one family member may handle medical coordination while another oversees finances. Identifying these roles during the initial conversation sets clear expectations.

3. **Extended Family or Support Network:** If other relatives or close friends will play a role in caregiving or financial support, consider including them in the discussion. Their input may be valuable, and their involvement can foster a stronger support network.

4. **Professional Advisors (Optional):** In some cases, involving professionals such as a family counselor, elder care manager, or financial planner in the conversation can provide clarity and impartiality. For example, a financial advisor could help explain the costs of various care options and how they align with the family's resources.

The presence of all relevant participants ensures transparency and allows for shared decision-making. However, it's essential to strike a balance between inclusivity and practicality. Too many voices in the room can make it difficult to focus and reach consensus.

## Goals and Follow-Up

Having clear goals for the conversation is essential to staying focused and achieving tangible outcomes. Before initiating the discussion, consider the objectives that need to be addressed. These goals might include understanding the care recipient's preferences, clarifying financial resources, or dividing caregiving responsibilities.

1. **Understand the Care Recipient's Wishes:** Begin by giving the person requiring care an opportunity to share their preferences. Do they want to remain in their home as long as possible, or are they open to assisted living options? What are their concerns about care, and what are their priorities for maintaining quality of life?

2. **Assess Family Perspectives:** Allow other participants to express their thoughts, concerns, and capabilities. This step ensures that each person's perspective is heard and considered. For example, one sibling may express concerns about balancing caregiving with their work schedule, while another may share ideas for financial contributions.

3. **Establish Immediate Priorities:** Identify any urgent needs or decisions that require immediate action. For instance, if the care recipient's mobility is declining, the family might prioritize making home modifications or securing in-home assistance.

4. **Outline Long-Term Plans:** Begin mapping out a framework for future care. While this conversation

doesn't need to resolve every detail, it should establish a starting point for ongoing planning. For example, the family might agree to research assisted living facilities or consult with a legal expert to update estate documents.

Once the initial goals are addressed, it's critical to establish a follow-up plan. A single conversation is rarely sufficient to address all aspects of long-term care planning. Follow-up plans might include scheduling additional family meetings, assigning research tasks, or consulting with professionals. Documenting key takeaways and action items helps keep everyone accountable and ensures that progress is made between discussions.
For example, after an initial meeting, the family could assign one person to gather information on in-home care providers and another to consult with a financial planner about Medicaid eligibility. A follow-up meeting could then be scheduled to review findings and make decisions based on the gathered information.

**Conclusion**
Starting the long-term care conversation is often the hardest step, but it is also the most critical. By carefully considering the timing, setting, participants, and goals, families can create an environment that fosters open communication and collaborative decision-making. Taking the time to plan these initial conversations thoughtfully ensures that future discussions and decisions are grounded in mutual understanding and shared purpose.

Ultimately, starting the conversation early allows families to address care needs proactively rather than reactively, ensuring that the care recipient's wishes are honored while reducing stress and conflict among family members. A well-executed approach sets the stage for effective planning and helps families navigate the complexities of long-term care with confidence.

## Conversation Topics

Having a structured framework for discussing long-term care needs is essential for productive and clear family conversations. Families often face challenges balancing personal wishes, financial realities, and medical and housing considerations while ensuring that all voices are heard. Breaking the discussion into specific topics allows everyone involved to focus on one issue at a time, reducing the emotional weight and potential for conflict. Below, we explore key areas to address during these conversations, ensuring a well-rounded and effective dialogue.

## Parent's Wishes and Concerns

The cornerstone of any long-term care conversation is understanding the wishes and concerns of the individual requiring care. While family members may have ideas about what's best, it's crucial to center the conversation around the preferences of the parent or loved one.

Start by asking open-ended questions to encourage the care recipient to share their thoughts. For example, "What are your priorities for your care as you age?" or "What's most important to you in terms of where and how you live?" These questions help establish their preferences regarding independence, privacy, and daily routines. For instance, one parent may express a strong desire to remain in their own home as long as possible, while another might feel more comfortable transitioning to an assisted living community for the social and medical support it provides.

Concerns about losing control or burdening family members often arise during these discussions. Acknowledging these emotions is important. Reassure the parent that the purpose of the conversation is to ensure their voice guides decisions and to create a plan that minimizes stress for everyone involved. Listening carefully to their fears, such as worries about financial strain or becoming a burden, helps families identify ways to address these issues proactively.

Families should also discuss cultural, religious, or personal values that may influence care preferences. For example, some parents may prioritize being close to family, while others might value access to specific community resources or activities. Addressing these concerns early ensures that the care plan reflects their unique identity and priorities.

## Financial Realities

One of the most challenging topics to discuss is the financial aspect of long-term care. However, addressing financial realities early is critical to creating a feasible care plan. The costs of care vary widely depending on the type and level of support needed. For instance, home care may cost $4,500 per month on average, while assisted living facilities can exceed $6,000 monthly, and nursing home care often costs upwards of $9,000 per month.

Start by reviewing the parent's financial resources. This includes savings, retirement accounts, Social Security benefits, pensions, and investments. It's essential to have a clear picture of available income streams and assets to determine how much care they can afford. Families should also discuss whether the parent has long-term care insurance or other coverage that could offset some costs.

Once the current financial situation is understood, families can begin exploring options for maximizing resources. For example, converting a life insurance policy to a long-term care benefit plan, establishing a trust, or leveraging home equity through a reverse mortgage are potential strategies. These discussions may also include creating a budget for future care expenses and determining how much financial support family members are willing or able to provide.
Financial planning should also address potential eligibility for government programs like Medicaid. Understanding Medicaid's asset and income limits and the five-year look-back period for asset transfers can help families make informed decisions about when to seek professional guidance.

## Medical and Housing Needs

Another critical topic to address is the parent's medical needs and housing preferences. These conversations should consider both current health conditions and potential future needs. For example, a parent with arthritis may require minor home modifications like grab bars or ramps in the short term, while someone with progressive cognitive decline may eventually need memory care services.

Start by reviewing the parent's current medical conditions, treatments, and medications. This provides a baseline for understanding their care needs and identifying gaps in their current support system. Discuss whether the parent prefers to remain at home or move to a facility when additional care is needed. For those who wish to stay in their home, families should explore options for in-home care services, adult day care, or home modifications to ensure safety and accessibility.

When discussing housing options, it's important to consider both emotional and logistical factors. For instance, transitioning to an assisted living community may offer opportunities for social engagement and access to medical staff, but it can also involve significant emotional adjustment. Families should weigh these factors alongside practical considerations, such as proximity to family members and availability of services.

It's also important to address contingency plans. What happens if the parent's health deteriorates unexpectedly? Establishing a clear timeline for reassessment and a plan for transitioning to higher levels of care ensures families are prepared for future changes.

**Professional Input**
Involving professionals can provide clarity, expertise, and impartial guidance during long-term care planning. Professionals bring specialized knowledge that can help families navigate complex issues such as legal requirements, financial strategies, and medical considerations.

## Elder Care Manager

An elder care manager, also known as a geriatric care manager, acts as a coordinator and advocate for the parent's needs. These professionals assess the parent's situation holistically, considering medical, financial, and personal factors. They can provide recommendations on care options, facilitate family discussions, and coordinate services such as in-home care or assisted living placement. For example, an elder care manager might help a family identify reputable in-home care providers, arrange transportation for medical appointments, and create a schedule for family caregivers. Their expertise ensures that care plans are comprehensive and tailored to the parent's unique needs.

## Legal and Financial Advisors

Legal and financial advisors play a critical role in addressing the technical aspects of long-term care planning. A qualified elder law attorney can assist with creating or updating essential documents, such as powers of attorney, healthcare directives, and wills. These documents ensure that the parent's wishes are legally documented and enforceable.

Additionally, financial advisors help families develop strategies to protect assets and maximize resources. For instance, they might recommend setting up an irrevocable trust to shield assets from Medicaid's asset limits or advise on tax-efficient ways to fund care expenses. Their guidance helps families navigate the financial complexities of long-term care while ensuring compliance with legal requirements.

## Medical Experts

Medical professionals provide essential input on the parent's care needs and options. A primary care physician can assess the parent's current health and provide recommendations for managing chronic conditions. Specialists, such as geriatricians or neurologists, may be consulted for more specific concerns, such as memory loss or mobility issues.

Medical experts also play a role in certifying the level of care needed for Medicaid or insurance eligibility. For example, a physician's certification may be required to document that the parent requires skilled nursing care or assistance with activities of daily living. Their expertise ensures that care plans are grounded in a clear understanding of the parent's medical needs.

**Conclusion**

Family conversations about long-term care are rarely easy, but addressing topics like personal wishes, financial realities, and medical needs in a structured way helps families navigate this complex process. Professional input from elder care managers, legal and financial advisors, and medical experts can further enhance these discussions by providing clarity and expertise. By taking the time to have open, honest conversations and leveraging professional guidance, families can create care plans that honor their parent's wishes, address practical realities, and provide peace of mind for everyone involved.

**Family Roles and Responsibilities**

When it comes to long-term care planning, clearly defining family roles and responsibilities is critical to ensure that everyone understands their contributions and expectations. Caregiving responsibilities can quickly become overwhelming without a structured approach, so it's important to allocate tasks thoughtfully and revisit them regularly to accommodate changes in needs or circumstances. This section explores the role of the primary caregiver, guided family discussions, and the importance of ongoing review and adjustments.

## Primary Caregiver Role

The primary caregiver often becomes the central figure in a family's long-term care strategy. This role typically requires a significant commitment of time, energy, and resources. Whether the caregiver is a spouse, adult child, or close relative, understanding the full scope of their duties is essential to avoid caregiver burnout and ensure the care recipient's needs are met.

## Time Commitment

Being a primary caregiver can be a full-time responsibility, especially as the care recipient's needs increase. The caregiver must often balance their personal and professional life while dedicating time to tasks like attending medical appointments, managing medications, and assisting with daily activities such as bathing, dressing, and meal preparation. A clear understanding of the time requirements upfront helps set realistic expectations and prevent overcommitment.

## Medical Coordination

Medical responsibilities are a major component of caregiving. The primary caregiver is typically tasked with coordinating doctor visits, managing prescriptions, and ensuring adherence to treatment plans. In cases involving chronic illnesses or memory impairments, these tasks can become even more demanding. For example, a caregiver for someone with dementia may need to monitor behavioral changes, administer medications, and communicate regularly with specialists.

## Financial Management

Caregiving often involves significant financial oversight. The primary caregiver may be responsible for managing the care recipient's budget, paying bills, and monitoring insurance claims. They may also need to make decisions about hiring professional caregivers, purchasing medical equipment, or funding assisted living arrangements. Transparent financial management and record-keeping are essential to avoid disputes or confusion among family members.

## Emotional Support

Providing emotional support is another key aspect of the primary caregiver's role. This involves offering companionship, listening to concerns, and fostering a sense of normalcy for the care recipient. However, caregivers must also recognize their own emotional limits and seek support when needed. Counseling, support groups, or respite care can help caregivers maintain their well-being while fulfilling this demanding role.

### Guided Discussions

Effective family discussions ensure that caregiving responsibilities are distributed fairly and that everyone has a clear understanding of their roles. Guided discussions help prevent misunderstandings and foster a collaborative approach to care planning.

## Role Assignments

Assigning roles based on each family member's strengths and availability is crucial. While one person may take on the primary caregiver role, others can contribute in complementary ways. For example, a sibling living nearby might assist with transportation to medical appointments, while another sibling living farther away could manage financial responsibilities or research care options. Clearly defining these roles reduces confusion and ensures no one feels unsupported or overburdened.

It's important to approach role assignments with empathy and open communication. Some family members may be unable to take on significant responsibilities due to work, health, or geographic constraints. Acknowledging these limitations and finding alternative ways for them to contribute ensures a fair distribution of duties.

## Emergency and End-of-Life Plans

Discussing emergency and end-of-life plans is an essential but often overlooked aspect of caregiving. Families should develop contingency plans for unexpected situations, such as the primary caregiver becoming unavailable or the care recipient experiencing a sudden health crisis. These plans might include identifying backup caregivers, creating a list of emergency contacts, and ensuring access to necessary medical information.

End-of-life planning is equally important. While these discussions can be emotionally difficult, they provide clarity and reduce stress during critical moments. Families should address topics like advance directives, hospice care preferences, and funeral arrangements. Documenting these decisions ensures they are honored and eliminates ambiguity during challenging times.

## Review and Adjustments

Caregiving needs and family circumstances often evolve over time, making regular reviews and adjustments a crucial part of the planning process. Ongoing communication ensures that the care plan remains effective and responsive to changing needs.

## Monthly and Annual Check-Ins

Regular check-ins provide an opportunity to assess the effectiveness of the current care plan and identify any emerging challenges. Monthly check-ins can focus on immediate concerns, such as scheduling conflicts, health updates, or financial needs. Annual assessments, on the other hand, allow families to evaluate long-term trends and make strategic adjustments. For example, an annual review might reveal the need to transition from in-home care to an assisted living facility or adjust financial strategies to cover increasing costs.

## Plan Updates and Role Changes

As care needs evolve, so too must the responsibilities of each family member. Plan updates may involve redistributing tasks, hiring additional support, or seeking professional guidance. For example, if the care recipient's medical condition worsens, the family might decide to hire a professional caregiver to assist with daily activities, allowing the primary caregiver to focus on coordination and emotional support.

Role changes can also occur due to shifting family dynamics. A sibling who was unable to contribute initially may later become available to take on a more active role, while another family member might need to reduce their involvement due to personal circumstances. Open communication and flexibility ensure that these transitions happen smoothly and without resentment.

Regular reviews also provide an opportunity to revisit financial and legal documents. Families should ensure that advance directives, powers of attorney, and care agreements remain up to date and reflect the care recipient's current needs and wishes. Keeping these documents current minimizes legal and logistical challenges during emergencies.

**Conclusion**

Family roles and responsibilities are the backbone of any successful long-term care plan. Clearly defining the primary caregiver's duties, facilitating guided discussions, and establishing regular review processes create a framework for effective collaboration and adaptability. While caregiving can be challenging, a well-structured approach ensures that responsibilities are shared fairly, and the care recipient's needs are met with compassion and consistency.

By assigning roles based on individual strengths, planning for emergencies and end-of-life situations, and maintaining open lines of communication, families can navigate the complexities of caregiving with confidence and resilience. Regular reviews and adjustments further strengthen the care plan, ensuring it remains responsive to changing circumstances and continues to provide the support and structure that everyone involved needs.

## Aging in Place Costs

Aging in place is an increasingly popular option for seniors who wish to remain in their homes rather than transitioning to a care facility. While this approach offers comfort, familiarity, and independence, it requires careful financial planning to cover the associated costs. Aging in place encompasses three primary categories of expenses: essential living expenses, healthcare-related costs, and support services. By understanding these expenses in detail, individuals and families can better prepare for the financial and logistical challenges of staying at home.

## Essential Living Expenses

Even when choosing to age in place, maintaining a home comes with ongoing costs. These include mortgage or rent payments, utilities, property taxes, and insurance, as well as regular maintenance and repairs.

### Mortgage or Rent

For those who own their home outright, aging in place can be relatively affordable. However, individuals with an outstanding mortgage must account for monthly payments in their financial planning. A typical mortgage payment for retirees ranges between $800 and $2,500 per month, depending on location and the remaining balance. For renters, monthly expenses might be similar or higher in areas with competitive housing markets. Planning ahead to pay off a mortgage before retirement, if possible, can significantly reduce financial stress when transitioning to a fixed income.

## Utilities and Maintenance

Utilities such as electricity, water, heating, and internet are ongoing expenses that can fluctuate with seasonal changes and the size of the home. On average, utility costs range between $150 and $400 monthly, depending on usage and energy efficiency. Maintenance expenses, including HVAC servicing, roof repairs, and plumbing fixes, can be less predictable but are essential for maintaining a safe and comfortable living environment. Budgeting for at least $1,000 annually for minor maintenance and having an emergency fund for larger repairs, such as a new roof or HVAC system, is critical.

## Property Taxes and Insurance

Property taxes vary widely depending on the location and assessed value of the home. Homeowners can expect to pay anywhere from 0.5% to 2% of their home's value annually. Retirees should be aware of property tax exemptions or reductions available to seniors in their area. Homeowners insurance is another essential cost, averaging $1,000 to $2,500 annually, depending on the home's size, location, and coverage level. For those in areas prone to natural disasters, additional coverage for floods, hurricanes, or earthquakes may be necessary, further increasing costs.

## Healthcare Expenses

Healthcare costs often become a significant financial burden as people age, particularly for those requiring ongoing or specialized care. Aging in place often involves in-home medical services, prescription management, and emergency response systems to ensure safety and well-being.

## In-Home Medical Services

For seniors requiring medical care, in-home services offer a convenient and often more comfortable alternative to facility-based care. Services can include visits from skilled nurses, physical or occupational therapy, and assistance with managing chronic conditions like diabetes or heart disease. The cost of in-home medical care varies based on the level of care needed. On average, a part-time home health aide costs $25 to $35 per hour, while skilled nursing care can cost $50 to $100 per hour. Monthly costs for in-home medical services may range from $1,000 to $5,000, depending on the frequency of visits and type of care required.

## Prescription Management

Managing medications is a critical component of healthcare for many seniors, particularly those with multiple chronic conditions. Costs can include the prescriptions themselves, which may range from $50 to $500 per month depending on insurance coverage, and services like automated prescription delivery or medication management systems. Some pharmacies and healthcare providers offer home delivery of prescriptions for a small monthly fee, often between $5 and $15. These services ensure that medications are delivered on time and reduce the burden on caregivers to pick up prescriptions.

## Emergency Response Systems

Investing in an emergency response system is essential for seniors aging in place, particularly those who live alone or have mobility challenges. These systems allow seniors to call for help at the push of a button in the event of a fall, medical emergency, or other urgent situation. Basic systems with a wearable button and 24/7 monitoring typically cost between $20 and $50 per month. Advanced systems with fall detection, GPS tracking, and smartphone integration may cost $50 to $100 monthly. While these systems represent an ongoing expense, they provide peace of mind for both seniors and their families.

## Support Services

Aging in place often requires supplemental support services to handle tasks that the senior may no longer be able to manage independently. Services such as meal delivery, housekeeping, and transportation play a vital role in maintaining quality of life.

## Meal Delivery

Preparing meals can become challenging for seniors with limited mobility, energy, or dexterity. Meal delivery services provide a solution by offering healthy, pre-prepared meals delivered directly to the home. Options range from programs like Meals on Wheels, which provide affordable or subsidized meals for seniors, to premium meal delivery services offering customized menus. Costs vary widely, with Meals on Wheels programs often charging $5 to $10 per meal, while private services may cost $10 to $15 per meal. Monthly costs can range from $150 to $500, depending on the frequency of deliveries and type of service selected.

## Housekeeping

Maintaining a clean and organized home is critical for health and safety, especially for seniors with mobility limitations or health conditions like asthma. Professional housekeeping services can include vacuuming, dusting, laundry, and kitchen cleaning. On average, a housekeeper costs $20 to $50 per hour, with a biweekly cleaning schedule costing $200 to $500 per month. For seniors on a budget, family members or local volunteer programs may provide assistance with housekeeping tasks at little or no cost.

## Transportation

For seniors who no longer drive, transportation services are essential for maintaining independence and accessing medical appointments, social activities, and shopping. Public transportation and senior transit programs often provide affordable options, though availability varies by location. Ride-sharing services like Uber and Lyft have also expanded to include senior-friendly options, with rides costing $10 to $30 depending on distance and time of day. Specialized medical transportation, such as wheelchair-accessible vans, may cost $50 to $100 per trip. Monthly transportation expenses typically range from $100 to $500, depending on frequency and type of service used.

**Conclusion**

Aging in place offers seniors the opportunity to remain in their homes and maintain their independence, but it comes with a variety of costs that must be carefully planned for. Essential living expenses such as mortgage payments, utilities, and property taxes form the foundation of the financial plan, while healthcare-related costs and support services address the unique needs of seniors as they age. By thoroughly understanding these expenses and creating a comprehensive budget, seniors and their families can ensure that aging in place remains a viable and comfortable option. Regularly reviewing and adjusting the budget is critical to addressing changes in needs and financial circumstances over time. With proper planning and resource allocation, aging in place can provide a safe, familiar, and fulfilling environment for seniors to enjoy their later years.

## Home Modification Budget

As seniors choose to age in place, modifying their homes to ensure safety and accessibility becomes an essential part of the planning process. Home modifications range from simple adjustments to significant renovations, depending on individual needs and the layout of the home. Developing a home modification budget ensures that all necessary changes are accounted for, reducing safety risks while enhancing mobility and independence.

## Safety Modifications

Safety modifications are the cornerstone of any home adaptation project for aging in place. These modifications aim to reduce fall risks and make navigating the home safer and more comfortable.

**Grab Bars**

Grab bars are one of the simplest yet most effective safety modifications. These bars provide support and stability, particularly in areas prone to slips and falls, such as bathrooms, hallways, and staircases. Grab bars are typically installed near toilets, bathtubs, and showers and can cost between $20 and $50 per bar, depending on material and design. Professional installation adds $100 to $300, depending on the location and wall type. For a comprehensive safety plan, installing grab bars throughout high-risk areas might cost $500 to $1,000.

**Ramps and Stair Lifts**

For seniors with mobility challenges, ramps and stair lifts are essential for navigating levels within and outside the home. Ramps allow wheelchair users or those with walkers to move freely, eliminating the need for steps. A basic wooden ramp costs $1,500 to $3,000, while aluminum or modular ramps with handrails can cost $2,000 to $5,000. For indoor stairs, stair lifts are a practical solution, costing between $3,000 and $10,000, depending on the length and complexity of the staircase. Although ramps and stair lifts are significant investments, they provide immediate benefits for individuals with mobility concerns and can significantly enhance accessibility.

### Improved Lighting

Adequate lighting is critical for preventing accidents, particularly for seniors with vision impairments. Enhancing lighting involves installing brighter bulbs, adding light fixtures in poorly lit areas, and using motion-sensor lights for convenience and safety. LED bulbs, which are energy-efficient and long-lasting, cost $5 to $15 each, while installing a motion-sensor light system typically costs $150 to $300 per fixture. Adding under-cabinet lighting in kitchens or stairway lights ensures high-risk areas are well-lit, with total costs ranging from $1,000 to $2,500, depending on the number of installations.

## Bathroom and Kitchen Adaptations

Bathrooms and kitchens are among the most frequently used areas in the home, making them high-priority spaces for aging-in-place modifications. Both spaces often require adjustments to improve accessibility, ensure safety, and accommodate physical limitations.

### Walk-in Tubs

Walk-in tubs provide a safer alternative to traditional bathtubs, which can be difficult for seniors to step in and out of. These tubs have a door that opens, allowing users to enter and exit with ease. They often include features such as built-in seating, anti-slip surfaces, and handrails. A basic walk-in tub costs between $2,000 and $5,000, while more advanced models with hydrotherapy features and fast-drain technology can cost up to $10,000. Installation costs range from $1,000 to $2,500, depending on plumbing and bathroom layout.

### Accessible Shelving

Accessible shelving ensures that frequently used items are within reach, reducing the need for bending, stretching, or climbing. This modification is particularly useful in kitchens, pantries, and closets. Pull-out shelves and lazy Susans are popular solutions that improve access to items stored in cabinets. Pull-out shelves cost $50 to $100 per shelf, while professionally installed systems range from $500 to $1,000 for a full kitchen. Pantry systems with adjustable shelving can cost $1,000 to $2,000. These upgrades enhance convenience and reduce the risk of injury caused by overexertion.

## Safety Features

Adding safety features in bathrooms and kitchens helps minimize accident risks and ensures that these spaces remain functional for individuals with physical limitations. Non-slip flooring is one of the most important safety upgrades. Materials such as textured vinyl, rubber, or non-slip ceramic tiles cost between $3 and $10 per square foot, with installation adding $1,000 to $2,500 for an average-sized bathroom. Anti-scald faucets and temperature regulators protect against burns, costing $50 to $200 per faucet. In kitchens, installing safety features such as stove shut-off devices and child-proof locks on cabinets can further enhance safety.

## Budgeting for Modifications

Creating a comprehensive budget for home modifications involves prioritizing changes based on safety needs and financial resources. Below is an example of potential costs for a typical aging-in-place project:

1. **Safety Modifications**

- Grab bars (5 installed): $500
- Improved lighting: $1,500
- Stair lift: $5,000
  **Subtotal:** $7,000

2. **Bathroom Adaptations**
   - Walk-in tub: $7,000
   - Non-slip flooring: $2,000
   - Anti-scald faucets: $300
     **Subtotal:** $9,300
3. **Kitchen Adaptations**
   - Accessible shelving: $1,500
   - Pull-out shelves: $800
   - Safety upgrades: $500
     **Subtotal:** $2,800

**Total Estimated Budget:** $19,100
Costs can vary significantly depending on the size of the home, the complexity of the modifications, and regional labor rates. Homeowners should also plan for a contingency fund of 10% to 20% of the total budget to account for unexpected expenses.

---

## Planning and Funding Modifications

Funding home modifications can be challenging, especially for seniors on a fixed income. However, several options can help alleviate the financial burden:

- **Medicaid Waivers**: In some states, Medicaid

provides funding for home modifications under waiver programs for seniors.

- **Veterans Benefits**: The Department of Veterans Affairs (VA) offers grants to eligible veterans for home modifications, including the Specially Adapted Housing (SAH) grant and Home Improvements and Structural Alterations (HISA) grant.
- **State and Local Programs**: Many state and local governments offer loans, grants, or tax credits for seniors making accessibility improvements.
- **Reverse Mortgages**: Seniors who own their homes outright or have significant equity may use a reverse mortgage to fund modifications.
- **Nonprofit Organizations**: Organizations like Rebuilding Together and Habitat for Humanity provide home repair assistance to seniors in need.

## Conclusion

Home modifications are an integral part of aging-in-place planning, ensuring safety, accessibility, and independence. Whether it's installing grab bars, upgrading lighting, or investing in a walk-in tub, each modification plays a vital role in creating a senior-friendly living environment. While costs can add up, thoughtful budgeting, prioritization, and exploring funding options can help make these necessary changes manageable. By proactively investing in home modifications, seniors and their families can enjoy peace of mind and a safer, more comfortable home environment.

## Caregiver Costs and Options

Planning for caregiver costs and exploring care options are vital steps in ensuring that long-term care needs are met while balancing financial, emotional, and logistical concerns. Whether relying on professional caregivers, family members, or a combination of both, understanding the associated costs, responsibilities, and planning strategies is essential for creating a sustainable care plan.

## Professional Care Services

Professional care services provide skilled and non-medical assistance to individuals who need help managing daily activities, recovering from illnesses, or living with chronic conditions. Each type of service comes with its own set of costs and benefits, catering to varying levels of care needs.

## Skilled Nursing

Skilled nursing services involve medical care provided by licensed nurses (RNs or LPNs) in the home or a facility setting. These services include wound care, administering medications, monitoring vital signs, and managing medical equipment like ventilators or feeding tubes. Skilled nursing is often necessary for individuals with complex medical conditions and post-hospitalization recovery needs.

The cost of skilled nursing care varies significantly depending on the level of care required and the setting. In 2025, the average cost for home-based skilled nursing services is approximately $75 to $150 per hour, while facility-based care in a nursing home costs between $250 and $500 per day. Medicare may cover skilled nursing services under specific circumstances, such as following a qualifying hospital stay, but long-term needs often require out-of-pocket funding or supplemental insurance.

## Personal Care Assistants

Personal care assistants (PCAs) provide non-medical assistance with daily activities such as bathing, dressing, grooming, meal preparation, and mobility support. PCAs enable individuals to maintain their independence and remain in their homes longer by offering essential support for activities of daily living (ADLs).

The average cost of hiring a personal care assistant is $20 to $35 per hour, with full-time services costing $4,000 to $6,000 per month. These services are usually not covered by Medicare, though Medicaid and long-term care insurance policies may provide some assistance. Many families rely on PCAs as part of a broader care plan that includes family involvement and professional oversight.

## Respite and Companion Care

Respite care provides temporary relief for primary caregivers, allowing them to take breaks, attend to personal responsibilities, or prevent burnout. Respite care can range from a few hours a week to several days or weeks, depending on the family's needs. Services may be provided in-home, at an adult day care center, or in a residential care facility. Costs for respite care vary but average $20 to $30 per hour for in-home services and $100 to $200 per day for facility-based care.

Companion care focuses on providing social interaction and light assistance rather than medical or personal care. Companions may help with errands, meal preparation, and transportation while offering emotional support. This type of care is particularly valuable for individuals experiencing loneliness or mild cognitive decline. Companion care costs typically range from $15 to $25 per hour, depending on location and services provided.

## Family Caregiver Needs

Family caregivers often play a central role in providing long-term care, but their contributions come with significant financial, emotional, and logistical challenges. Recognizing and addressing the needs of family caregivers is critical to maintaining their well-being and ensuring effective care delivery.

## Financial Impact

Family caregivers frequently face financial sacrifices, including reduced work hours, lost wages, and out-of-pocket expenses for care-related items. According to recent studies, the average family caregiver spends $7,000 annually on expenses such as medical supplies, transportation, and home modifications. For caregivers who reduce their work hours or leave the workforce entirely, the long-term financial impact can be even greater, affecting retirement savings and future Social Security benefits.

To mitigate the financial strain, families should explore compensation options such as caregiver agreements, Medicaid's Cash and Counseling programs, and state-specific caregiver support initiatives. Creating a formal care contract that outlines payment terms, duties, and expectations can help clarify financial arrangements and ensure fairness among family members.

## Burnout Prevention

Caregiving can be emotionally and physically demanding, leading to burnout if proper support and self-care strategies are not in place. Common signs of caregiver burnout include fatigue, irritability, depression, and declining physical health. Preventing burnout requires a proactive approach that includes:

- **Respite Care**: Utilizing professional respite services to take regular breaks.

- **Support Networks**: Joining caregiver support groups to connect with others in similar situations.

- **Time Management**: Setting boundaries and

prioritizing personal time.

- **Professional Counseling**: Seeking therapy to address emotional challenges.

Family caregivers should also consider creating a care team that distributes responsibilities among multiple family members or professional caregivers, reducing the burden on any one individual.

## Tax Benefits

Family caregivers may qualify for tax benefits to help offset care-related costs. These include:

- **Dependent Care Tax Credit**: Caregivers supporting elderly dependents may claim a portion of care expenses as a tax credit, subject to income limits.

- **Medical Expense Deductions**: Caregivers can deduct qualifying medical expenses that exceed 7.5% of their adjusted gross income.

- **Flexible Spending Accounts (FSAs)**: Some caregivers can use FSA funds to pay for eligible care expenses.

- **Caregiver Stipends**: In some cases, Medicaid or veterans' benefits programs may provide financial assistance to family caregivers.

Working with a tax professional can help caregivers maximize these benefits while ensuring compliance with IRS regulations.

## Care Scheduling

Effective scheduling is crucial for ensuring that caregiving responsibilities are managed efficiently and flexibly. Families must decide whether full-time, part-time, or hybrid care arrangements best suit their needs and explore options for emergency and backup coverage.

### Full-Time vs. Part-Time Care

Full-time care is often necessary for individuals with advanced medical needs or significant limitations in daily activities. This level of care typically involves a combination of professional caregivers, family involvement, and support services. Full-time care can cost $8,000 to $12,000 per month, depending on the type of care and location.

Part-time care is ideal for individuals who need occasional assistance or support during specific times of the day, such as mornings or evenings. Part-time care costs vary but generally range from $2,000 to $4,000 per month for 20 to 30 hours of weekly care. Families often combine part-time professional care with family caregiving to balance costs and responsibilities.

## Backup and Emergency Plans

Care plans must include contingencies for unexpected situations such as caregiver illness, emergencies, or changes in care needs. Creating a backup plan ensures continuity of care and minimizes disruptions. Key components of a backup plan include:

- **Emergency Caregivers**: Identifying trusted family members, friends, or professional services that can step in during emergencies.

- **Care Directories**: Maintaining a list of local home care agencies, respite services, and adult day care centers.
- **Emergency Kits**: Preparing kits with essential medical information, medications, and contact details for quick access.
- **Flexible Scheduling**: Arranging overlapping schedules among caregivers to ensure coverage during unexpected absences.

Planning for emergencies requires open communication among family members and clear documentation of care preferences and medical needs. Families should review and update their backup plans annually or after significant changes in circumstances.

**Conclusion**

Caregiver costs and options are diverse, requiring thoughtful planning to balance financial, emotional, and logistical considerations. Professional care services, including skilled nursing, personal care assistants, and respite care, offer valuable support but come at a financial cost. Family caregivers play a crucial role but face unique challenges that must be addressed through financial planning, burnout prevention strategies, and tax benefits. Finally, effective care scheduling, including backup and emergency plans, ensures that caregiving responsibilities are managed efficiently and flexibly. By understanding and integrating these elements, families can create a comprehensive caregiving plan that meets the needs of both care recipients and caregivers, ensuring quality care and peace of mind.

# Chapter 7: Facility Care Options

As individuals age, the decision to transition from home care to a facility-based care option can be challenging. Choosing the right facility requires careful evaluation of the available options, services provided, and how each facility meets medical, social, and personal care needs. In this chapter, we'll explore three of the most common types of care facilities: independent living communities, assisted living facilities, and memory care units. Understanding the unique features and offerings of each type can help families and individuals make informed decisions that align with their needs and preferences.

## Types of Care Facilities

## Independent Living Communities

Independent living communities cater to seniors who are generally healthy and capable of managing daily activities without intensive medical or personal care. These communities offer a blend of housing, services, and amenities designed to promote an active and fulfilling lifestyle for older adults.

### Services and Amenities

Independent living communities typically provide private or semi-private apartments and condominiums equipped with features such as emergency call systems, easy-to-navigate layouts, and low-maintenance living spaces. In addition to housing, these communities offer various services that enhance convenience and quality of life, including:

- **Housekeeping and Laundry**: Regular cleaning and linen services reduce the physical burden of household chores.
- **Meal Plans and Dining Options**: On-site dining facilities provide nutritious meals, often tailored to dietary restrictions.
- **Transportation Services**: Scheduled shuttles and ride services facilitate access to medical appointments, shopping, and recreational activities.
- **Maintenance and Repairs**: Routine maintenance ensures residents live in a safe and functional environment.

These services provide seniors with the freedom to focus on activities they enjoy rather than worrying about household management.

## Social and Lifestyle Programs

One of the main attractions of independent living communities is their emphasis on social engagement and wellness. Many communities offer structured programs to help residents stay physically active, mentally stimulated, and socially connected. Examples of such programs include:

- **Fitness Classes**: Yoga, tai chi, and water aerobics classes encourage physical fitness and mobility.
- **Clubs and Interest Groups**: Book clubs, gardening groups, and hobby workshops provide opportunities for residents to pursue their interests.

- **Educational Seminars**: Regular lectures on topics like financial planning, health management, and technology use help residents stay informed.
- **Community Events**: Game nights, holiday parties, and cultural outings foster camaraderie among residents.

For active seniors seeking an environment that promotes independence and socialization, independent living communities offer a balanced blend of convenience and engagement.

## Assisted Living Facilities

Assisted living facilities are designed for individuals who require assistance with activities of daily living (ADLs), such as bathing, dressing, or medication management, but do not need the round-the-clock medical care provided in nursing homes. These facilities offer a supportive environment that encourages independence while ensuring access to necessary care.

## Care Levels and Medical Support

Assisted living facilities provide tiered care levels, which can be customized based on the resident's evolving needs. These levels often range from light assistance to more intensive support, ensuring that residents receive the right level of care without overpaying for unneeded services. Key medical support services offered in assisted living facilities include:

- **Medication Management**: Staff ensures that residents take their prescribed medications correctly and on schedule.

- **On-Site Health Services**: Some facilities have visiting doctors, nurses, or therapists who provide routine checkups, physical therapy, or other health-related services.
- **Emergency Response Systems**: Facilities are equipped with call buttons, wearable devices, and on-site staff trained to respond to medical emergencies.
- **Memory Support Services**: Many assisted living facilities offer specialized care for residents in the early stages of dementia or cognitive decline.

These services ensure that residents receive adequate medical care in a safe and supportive environment, even as their needs change over time.

## Personal Services and Activities

In addition to medical support, assisted living facilities prioritize personal care and social enrichment. Staff members are available to assist residents with ADLs, such as:

- **Bathing and Grooming**: Ensuring residents maintain personal hygiene and dignity.
- **Meal Assistance**: Helping those with physical limitations eat or prepare meals.
- **Mobility Support**: Assisting with wheelchairs, walkers, and transfers.

The activities provided at assisted living facilities focus on maintaining physical, emotional, and social well-being. Examples include:

- **Group Outings**: Trips to museums, theaters, and

parks encourage social interaction.

- **Recreational Activities**: Games, arts and crafts, and movie nights provide entertainment and engagement.
- **Therapeutic Sessions**: Programs like music therapy, pet therapy, and mindfulness exercises promote mental health and relaxation.

By balancing medical care with personalized support and social activities, assisted living facilities create an environment where residents can thrive.

## Memory Care Units

Memory care units are specialized facilities designed to meet the needs of individuals with Alzheimer's disease, dementia, or other cognitive impairments. These units offer a secure and structured environment with staff trained to manage the unique challenges associated with memory loss.

## Security and Safety Features

One of the primary concerns for individuals with memory impairments is safety. Memory care units address these concerns through the implementation of advanced security measures, such as:

- **Secured Entrances and Exits**: Controlled access prevents residents from wandering outside the facility unsupervised.
- **Alarm Systems**: Motion detectors and alarms monitor residents' movements to ensure their safety.

- **Emergency Call Systems**: Easily accessible call buttons allow residents to summon help when needed.

Additionally, the physical layout of memory care units is designed to reduce confusion and promote a sense of calm. Features like color-coded hallways, clear signage, and circular floor plans minimize disorientation and make it easier for residents to navigate their surroundings.

## Specialized Staff and Programs

The staff in memory care units undergo specialized training to address the behavioral, emotional, and medical needs of residents with cognitive impairments. Key aspects of staff training include:

- **Communication Techniques**: Learning how to engage with residents in a way that fosters understanding and reduces anxiety.
- **Behavioral Management**: Recognizing and responding to signs of agitation, confusion, or aggression.
- **Care Personalization**: Developing individualized care plans based on the resident's history, preferences, and needs.

Programs offered in memory care units are tailored to stimulate cognitive function, promote emotional well-being, and maintain a sense of routine. Examples include:

- **Reminiscence Therapy**: Activities that encourage residents to recall and share past experiences, helping to preserve memories and foster connections.

- **Sensory Stimulation**: Activities like aromatherapy, music therapy, and tactile games engage the senses and provide comfort.
- **Structured Daily Schedules**: Consistent routines reduce confusion and create a sense of stability for residents.

Family involvement is also emphasized in memory care units. Regular meetings with staff, support groups, and educational sessions help families understand the progression of memory loss and how to support their loved ones effectively.

**Conclusion**

Choosing the right type of care facility requires a careful assessment of the individual's needs, preferences, and financial resources. Independent living communities offer active seniors the opportunity to enjoy a maintenance-free lifestyle with ample social opportunities. Assisted living facilities provide the perfect balance of independence and support for individuals requiring help with daily activities and medical needs. Memory care units deliver specialized care and security for those living with cognitive impairments, ensuring their safety and dignity. Each facility type plays a critical role in addressing the diverse care needs of aging adults. By understanding the services, amenities, and programs offered at each level, families can make informed decisions that promote the health, happiness, and well-being of their loved ones.

## Skilled Nursing Facilities

Skilled nursing facilities (SNFs) are an integral part of the long-term care landscape, offering a higher level of medical and personal care than other facility types. They cater to individuals with complex medical needs that require round-the-clock supervision, specialized rehabilitation services, or long-term care for chronic conditions. These facilities are staffed by licensed medical professionals, including nurses, therapists, and physicians, ensuring that residents receive the highest standard of care tailored to their specific needs.

## Medical and Rehabilitation Services

One of the primary functions of skilled nursing facilities is to provide advanced medical care and rehabilitation services. These services are designed for individuals recovering from surgeries, injuries, or acute medical conditions, as well as those managing chronic illnesses.

**Comprehensive Medical Care** Skilled nursing facilities offer 24-hour medical supervision to monitor and manage residents' health. Physicians typically oversee care plans, while registered nurses (RNs) and licensed practical nurses (LPNs) administer medications, manage wound care, and monitor vital signs. This level of care ensures that residents with complex medical needs, such as those with ventilators, feeding tubes, or dialysis requirements, receive continuous and attentive support.

Residents in skilled nursing facilities also benefit from regular medical evaluations and preventive care measures, such as vaccinations, chronic disease management, and mental health support. This proactive approach helps prevent health deterioration and promotes overall well-being.

**Rehabilitation Services** Rehabilitation is a core focus of skilled nursing facilities, often making them a transitional care option after hospital stays. Facilities provide physical, occupational, and speech therapy services tailored to residents' recovery goals.

- **Physical Therapy**: Designed to improve mobility, strength, and balance, physical therapy helps residents regain independence after surgeries like hip replacements or recover from conditions like strokes.

- **Occupational Therapy**: Occupational therapists focus on helping residents relearn essential daily activities, such as dressing, eating, and bathing, ensuring they can maintain as much autonomy as possible.

- **Speech Therapy**: Speech therapists address communication challenges and swallowing difficulties, often a result of strokes, neurological disorders, or degenerative conditions.

These therapies are typically administered through individualized treatment plans that evolve as residents progress. A collaborative approach among therapists, physicians, and caregivers ensures that care remains aligned with the resident's health and functional goals.

## Long-Term Care Options

While many residents enter skilled nursing facilities for short-term rehabilitation, others require long-term care due to chronic conditions, advanced age, or disabilities that make independent living untenable. Long-term care services in SNFs are designed to provide ongoing medical, emotional, and personal support.

**Chronic Condition Management** For residents with chronic illnesses such as Parkinson's disease, heart failure, or advanced diabetes, skilled nursing facilities provide comprehensive management plans. This includes medication administration, monitoring for complications, and implementing lifestyle adjustments to improve residents' quality of life.

**Palliative and Hospice Care** For residents facing terminal illnesses or significant pain, skilled nursing facilities often provide palliative and hospice care. These services focus on enhancing comfort, relieving symptoms, and supporting emotional well-being. Family members are also included in care plans to ensure they feel supported throughout the process.

**Specialized Units** Many skilled nursing facilities have specialized units to cater to residents with specific conditions. Memory care wings are common, offering secure environments and tailored activities for individuals with dementia or Alzheimer's disease. Other facilities may have bariatric units, ventilator care units, or units designed for individuals with complex neurological conditions.

**Daily Living Assistance** In addition to medical and rehabilitative care, skilled nursing facilities offer assistance with daily living activities, such as bathing, dressing, eating, and mobility. Caregivers are trained to provide compassionate support while respecting residents' dignity and privacy.

## Continuing Care Retirement Communities (CCRCs)

Continuing care retirement communities (CCRCs) represent a unique and comprehensive approach to senior living. They provide a continuum of care within a single community, allowing residents to transition seamlessly between different care levels as their needs evolve. CCRCs typically include independent living, assisted living, skilled nursing, and sometimes memory care facilities, all on one campus. This integrated model offers significant advantages in terms of convenience, consistency, and peace of mind for both residents and their families.

**Care Transitions and Financial Structure**
One of the defining features of CCRCs is their ability to accommodate changing care needs without requiring residents to leave the community. This flexibility is especially appealing for seniors seeking long-term stability in their living arrangements.

**Seamless Care Transitions** In CCRCs, residents can move between independent living, assisted living, and skilled nursing care as their health needs change. For example, a resident may begin in an independent living apartment but transition to assisted living if they require help with daily activities. If their health further declines, they can access skilled nursing care or memory care without the upheaval of relocating to a different facility.

This seamless transition process ensures continuity of care, as the same community staff and medical teams often oversee residents throughout their journey. It also fosters a sense of familiarity and stability, which is particularly beneficial for seniors with cognitive impairments or chronic illnesses.

**Financial Structure** The financial arrangements of CCRCs can be complex, but they are designed to provide residents with predictability and security. Typically, CCRCs require an upfront entry fee in addition to monthly service fees. The entry fee can range from $100,000 to over $1 million, depending on the community, residence size, and care package selected.
Monthly fees vary based on the level of care and amenities provided. Independent living residents generally pay lower monthly fees, while those in skilled nursing or memory care units pay higher rates to reflect the additional services they receive.

There are several contract models commonly used in CCRCs:

- **Type A (Life Care Contracts)**: Residents pay a higher entry fee and monthly rate, but their costs remain stable even if they transition to higher levels of care. This model provides the greatest financial predictability.

- **Type B (Modified Contracts)**: These contracts offer lower entry and monthly fees but include limitations on how much care is covered. Residents may pay additional fees if they require extensive medical or personal care.

- **Type C (Fee-for-Service Contracts)**: Residents pay for services and care as they need them, resulting in lower upfront costs but potentially higher expenses over time.

The financial structure of CCRCs allows families to plan for future care costs with greater certainty. However, it's essential to carefully evaluate contract terms, refund policies, and the community's financial stability before making a commitment.

## Entry and Contract Requirements

Joining a CCRC involves several steps, including meeting entry requirements, selecting a contract type, and planning for the long-term financial implications. Understanding these requirements is crucial for families considering this option.

**Entry Requirements** Most CCRCs have specific criteria that prospective residents must meet before admission. These requirements typically include:

- **Age**: Many CCRCs have a minimum age requirement, often 62 or older.

- **Health Assessments**: Applicants may need to

undergo medical evaluations to ensure they meet the health criteria for independent or assisted living.

- **Financial Eligibility**: CCRCs often require prospective residents to demonstrate that they have sufficient assets or income to cover the entry fee and monthly fees over the long term.

These criteria are designed to ensure that residents can fully participate in and benefit from the community's services.

**Contract Selection** Choosing the right contract is a critical step in joining a CCRC. Families should carefully evaluate the options available and consider factors such as:

- **Care Needs**: Residents with existing medical conditions may benefit from a Type A contract, which provides stable costs for higher levels of care.

- **Budget**: Type C contracts offer lower initial costs but require careful planning for future care expenses.

- **Legacy Goals**: Some contracts offer partial or full refunds of entry fees, which can be passed on to heirs.

**Planning for the Future** When evaluating CCRCs, it's essential to consider the community's reputation, financial health, and quality of care. Touring the facilities, speaking with current residents, and reviewing state inspection reports can provide valuable insights.

Additionally, families should work with financial advisors and elder care attorneys to ensure they understand the long-term financial implications of joining a CCRC. Proper planning can help mitigate risks and ensure that residents can comfortably afford the care they need.

**Conclusion**

Skilled nursing facilities and continuing care retirement communities are two vital options for seniors requiring advanced care and long-term support. Skilled nursing facilities excel in providing intensive medical and rehabilitative services, making them ideal for individuals recovering from serious health events or managing chronic conditions. In contrast, CCRCs offer a comprehensive and flexible living arrangement that allows residents to transition seamlessly between care levels, providing peace of mind and stability.

Understanding the unique features, services, and financial structures of these facilities empowers families to make informed decisions that align with their loved ones' needs and goals. Whether choosing a skilled nursing facility for short-term recovery or a CCRC for long-term stability, these care options play a crucial role in promoting the health, well-being, and quality of life of older adults.

## Conclusion: The Path to Preparedness and Peace of Mind

The journey through long-term care planning, as outlined in this book, serves as a roadmap for navigating one of the most complex challenges of aging. From understanding care options and funding strategies to starting critical family conversations, every step we've discussed reinforces the same fundamental truth: preparation is not optional. It's essential.

### A Look Back: The Core Lessons Learned

**The Necessity of Proactive Planning** We've explored the many facets of long-term care planning—from understanding care needs and facility options to engaging in critical family conversations. Each step reinforces the need for early and deliberate action. The stories of individuals like Sarah, who struggled to cover care costs unexpectedly, highlight the financial and emotional burdens that unprepared families often face. On the other hand, those who planned early found themselves in better control, with the ability to adapt to changes without compromising their financial stability.

**Funding Long-Term Care: Exploring the Options** One of the central themes of this book has been the variety of ways to fund long-term care. From self-funding strategies to private insurance and Medicaid planning, each option offers unique benefits and challenges. However, for many, these methods can be unpredictable or restrictive. Traditional insurance, for example, often comes with "use it or lose it" risks and rising premiums. Self-funding demands substantial financial discipline and may deplete assets intended for heirs.

Enter long-term care annuities—an option that combines financial security with remarkable flexibility. These products are designed to address the concerns that other funding methods cannot, offering a predictable, guaranteed stream of benefits while allowing individuals to maintain access to their funds.

**The New Reality of Long-Term Care** We began this journey by addressing the growing need for long-term care and the challenges facing traditional retirement planning methods. Longevity, rising care costs, and shrinking family support networks have made long-term care a cornerstone of modern retirement planning. The stories of individuals like Bob, Linda, and Maria illustrated the stark realities families face without adequate preparation. Their experiences underscore the importance of addressing these needs early, holistically, and proactively.

**Facility and Home Care Options** Knowing the types of care available is essential for making informed decisions. From independent living communities to skilled nursing facilities, each option comes with its own benefits, costs, and considerations. For those preferring to age in place, home modifications and in-home care services offer viable alternatives. These insights empower families to weigh the pros and cons of various arrangements and choose the best fit for their needs.

**The Importance of Communication** One of the most overlooked aspects of planning is the need for open and honest family conversations. Discussing care preferences, assigning roles, and addressing financial realities are difficult but necessary steps. Families that engage in these discussions early are better equipped to navigate crises and make unified decisions when the time comes.

**Medicaid and Legal Considerations** For those relying on Medicaid, understanding eligibility requirements and the role of legal documents like trusts, powers of attorney, and healthcare directives is crucial. These tools not only protect assets but also ensure that care preferences are honored, reducing stress during emotionally charged times.

**The Cost of Inaction**

The financial and emotional toll of neglecting long-term care planning cannot be overstated. Families who delay planning often find themselves unprepared to handle crises, leading to rushed decisions, strained relationships, and financial hardship. Consider the stories of Sarah, who became a caregiver overnight, or the Martinez family, who were blindsided by Medicare's coverage gaps. Their experiences highlight the risks of reactive planning and the peace of mind that comes from proactive measures.

**Taking the First Step**

The first step in long-term care planning is often the hardest. It requires acknowledging the possibility of future care needs and confronting difficult questions about aging, independence, and family roles. But as we've seen throughout this book, taking that first step is also the most important. It sets the stage for a comprehensive plan that protects not just financial stability but also emotional well-being.

**A Framework for Action**

To help you get started, here's a step-by-step framework for long-term care planning:

1. **Assess Your Situation**
    - Evaluate your health, family history, and lifestyle to estimate your potential care needs.
    - Review your financial resources, including savings, insurance, and retirement accounts.

2. **Educate Yourself**
   - Understand the types of care available and the costs associated with each.
   - Learn about Medicare, Medicaid, and other public programs, as well as private insurance options.
3. **Engage Your Family**
   - Discuss your care preferences and expectations with your loved ones.
   - Assign roles and responsibilities to avoid confusion and conflict later.
4. **Create a Financial Plan**
   - Explore funding options, including self-funding, insurance products, and government programs.
   - Work with financial and legal advisors to optimize your strategy.
5. **Prepare Legal Documents**
   - Establish or update your will, powers of attorney, and healthcare directives.
   - Consider trusts or other tools to protect assets and ensure your wishes are honored.
6. **Plan for Transitions**
   - Identify potential care facilities or services in your area.

- Create a contingency plan for unexpected health changes or emergencies.

7. **Review and Adjust**

    - Revisit your plan annually or after major life events to ensure it remains aligned with your needs and goals.

**The Power of Planning**

Proper long-term care planning is about more than money—it's about peace of mind. It's about knowing that your needs will be met without placing undue burden on your loved ones. It's about maintaining dignity and independence, even in the face of life's uncertainties.

Throughout this book, we've provided the tools and knowledge you need to take control of your future. Whether you're just starting to think about long-term care or refining an existing plan, the key is to take action. Every step you take now reduces the risk of stress and hardship later.

**A Call to Action**

As you close this book, consider what steps you can take today to secure your tomorrow. Whether it's scheduling a meeting with a financial advisor, discussing care preferences with your family, or researching local care providers, every action brings you closer to a comprehensive plan.

Remember, the goal of long-term care planning is not to predict the future but to prepare for it. By taking proactive steps, you can face whatever comes with confidence and clarity, knowing that you've done everything possible to protect yourself and your loved ones.

**Final Thoughts**

Long-term care planning is one of the most compassionate acts you can undertake—for yourself and for those who love you. It's a journey that requires honesty, diligence, and courage, but the rewards are immeasurable. By preparing now, you give yourself the gift of peace of mind and the ability to focus on what truly matters: living your life to the fullest.

Thank you for joining me on this journey. May this book serve as a guide and a source of inspiration as you take the steps necessary to secure your future. The path to preparedness and peace of mind begins with you—and it begins today.

## Glossary of Terms

1. **Activities of Daily Living (ADLs):** Basic self-care tasks like bathing, dressing, eating, and toileting, often used to determine eligibility for long-term care services.
2. **Adult Foster Care:** Small group homes providing personal care and supervision in a residential setting.
3. **Annuity:** A financial product providing regular payments over a specified period, often used in retirement planning.
4. **Asset Protection:** Strategies to shield personal assets from long-term care costs or creditors.
5. **Assisted Living Waiver:** A Medicaid program covering some costs of assisted living for eligible individuals.
6. **Benefit Trigger:** The criteria that must be met for an insurance policy to begin paying benefits, often related to the inability to perform ADLs.
7. **Caregiver Burnout:** Physical, emotional, and mental exhaustion experienced by caregivers.
8. **Chronic Condition:** A long-lasting health issue requiring ongoing care, such as diabetes or arthritis.
9. **Claim Waiting Period:** The time a policyholder

must wait before receiving benefits after filing a claim.

10. **Community-Based Care:** Services provided outside of institutions, such as adult day care or home health services.
11. **Death Benefit:** The payout from a life insurance policy to beneficiaries upon the insured's death.
12. **Deferred Annuity:** A retirement product that delays payouts until a future date.
13. **Disability Insurance:** A policy replacing income lost due to the inability to work from injury or illness.
14. **Elder Law Attorney:** A lawyer specializing in legal issues affecting seniors, such as Medicaid planning and estate planning.
15. **Elimination Period:** The waiting time before an insurance policy begins paying benefits after qualifying.
16. **Estate Planning:** Organizing finances and assets for distribution after death.
17. **Family Caregiver Agreement:** A formal contract outlining compensation for family members providing care.
18. **Federal Poverty Level (FPL):** A measure used to determine Medicaid and other assistance eligibility.
19. **Financial Power of Attorney:** A document appointing someone to manage financial affairs if

the individual is unable to do so.

20. **Flexible Spending Account (FSA):** A pre-tax account used for healthcare expenses, including some caregiving costs.
21. **Health Savings Account (HSA):** A tax-advantaged account for medical expenses, often used alongside high-deductible health plans.
22. **Home Equity Conversion Mortgage (HECM):** A type of reverse mortgage allowing seniors to access home equity for expenses.
23. **Home Modification:** Changes made to a home to accommodate mobility or safety needs, such as ramps or grab bars.
24. **Hospice Care:** End-of-life care focused on comfort rather than curative treatments.
25. **Hybrid Annuity:** A financial product combining annuity benefits with long-term care coverage.
26. **Indexed Universal Life (IUL):** A life insurance policy with cash value growth tied to stock market indexes.
27. **Independent Living Facility:** A residential community for active seniors requiring minimal assistance.
28. **Inflation Adjustment:** A feature in financial products to account for rising costs over time.
29. **Irrevocable Trust:** A trust that cannot be modified without the beneficiary's consent, often

used for Medicaid planning.

30. **Joint and Survivor Annuity:** An annuity providing income to a spouse after the primary annuitant's death.

31. **Managed Care Plan:** A health insurance plan emphasizing network-based services and cost control.

32. **Means-Tested Program:** Benefits requiring income or asset limits for eligibility, such as Medicaid.

33. **Medicaid Spend-Down:** Reducing assets to qualify for Medicaid benefits.

34. **Memory Care Facility:** A specialized facility for individuals with Alzheimer's or other cognitive impairments.

35. **Multigenerational Housing:** Living arrangements where multiple generations share a home to reduce costs and provide support.

36. **Non-Covered Services:** Healthcare services not paid for by Medicare, Medicaid, or private insurance.

37. **PACE (Program of All-Inclusive Care for the Elderly):** A program providing comprehensive care to seniors eligible for nursing home-level services.

38. **Part A (Medicare):** Covers hospital stays, skilled nursing facilities, and some home healthcare

services.

39. **Part B (Medicare):** Covers outpatient services, preventive care, and medical equipment.

40. **Part D (Medicare):** Provides prescription drug coverage.

41. **Qualified Longevity Annuity Contract (QLAC):** An annuity exempt from Required Minimum Distributions, providing income later in life.

42. **Rehabilitation Services:** Short-term care helping individuals recover physical or cognitive abilities after an injury or illness.

43. **Required Minimum Distribution (RMD):** The minimum withdrawal amount retirees must take from certain retirement accounts annually.

44. **Reverse Mortgage:** A loan allowing seniors to access home equity without monthly repayments.

45. **Risk Pooling:** Insurance concept spreading financial risk across many policyholders.

46. **Sequence of Returns Risk:** The danger of withdrawing from retirement accounts during market downturns, depleting assets prematurely.

47. **Skilled Nursing Facility (SNF):** A licensed facility providing 24-hour medical care.

48. **Tax-Free Growth:** Investment earnings not subject to taxation, as in Roth accounts.

49. **Trustee:** The person or institution managing assets in a trust.

50. **Turnkey Care Solutions:** Comprehensive packages covering all aspects of senior care.

51. **Underwriting:** The process insurers use to assess risk and determine policy terms.

52. **Uniform Transfers to Minors Act (UTMA):** A law allowing property transfer to minors without a formal trust.

53. **Voluntary Caregiver Agreement:** A contract where informal caregivers provide services for a negotiated fee.

54. **Wealth Preservation Trust:** A trust designed to protect assets from being depleted by long-term care costs.

55. **Will:** A legal document stating how a person's assets should be distributed after death.

56. **Wraparound Coverage:** Supplemental insurance designed to fill gaps in primary coverage.

For Additional Support:

We are here to help. Request your free Social Security Analysis and retirement Income Plan. If you would like personalized guidance in maximizing your Social Security benefits and creating a comprehensive retirement income strategy, please contact:

Boom Retirement Solutions
(888) 839-1611

**SCAN TO SCHEDULE**

**AN APPOINTMENT**

For a free copy of our other book "Maximizing Social Security Benefits" send an email to **jeff@boomretirement.com** and in the Subject Line write "Free Book Social Security."

Made in the USA
Las Vegas, NV
14 June 2026

48873871R00141